Presented to

_____

By

_____

On the Occasion of

_____

Date

_____

TEACHER TO TEACHER

Inspiring Devotions

for Educators

Dorothy Howell Robinson

BARBOUR BOOKS
An Imprint of Barbour Publishing, Inc.

© 2001 by Dorothy Robinson.

ISBN 1-58660-237-3

Scripture taken from the HOLY BIBLE, NEW INTERNATIONAL VERSION®. NIV®. Copyright © 1973, 1978, 1984 by International Bible Society. Used by permission of Zondervan Publishing House. All rights reserved.

Published by Barbour Books, an imprint of Barbour Publishing, Inc., P.O. Box 719, Uhrichsville, Ohio 44683, www.barbourbooks.com

ecpa Member of the
Evangelical Christian
Publishers Association

Printed in the United States of America.

CONTENTS

INTRODUCTION

The ideas for this book have been coming to me in flashes for several years. As I learned about spiritual gifts and recognized that God has given me the gift of encouragement and an ability to write, I realized that God was leading me to write these devotionals.

While the devotionals are applicable for any Christian, I felt they were given to me to be shared with members of a very beleaguered and disheartened profession—teachers. Having recently retired from teaching after twenty-six years, both as a general curriculum teacher and as a special education teacher, I am acutely aware of the daily frustrations and demands of the teaching profession.

I have written this book as God has led me, and I trust Him to see this through to completion. May the Lord bless these words and use them to encourage others in their spiritual journey.

DOT HOWELL ROBINSON

*Now to him who is able to do
immeasurably more than all
we ask or imagine,
according to his power
that is at work within us,
to him be glory in the church
and in Christ Jesus throughout
all generations, for ever and ever! Amen.*
EPHESIANS 3:20–21

ACKNOWLEDGMENTS

I thank God for setting these words upon my heart and giving me the gift of writing. This book was written to glorify God and to encourage friends in the faith. Such a learning experience has challenged me in my Bible study and daily walk with the Lord.

I owe a tremendous debt of gratitude to my husband, Joe, and our son, Ben, who have been so supportive and patient during the process of writing. For all the days the house didn't get cleaned and you ate leftovers for dinner, thanks for understanding. Ben, thanks for being my technical adviser. Without your help, guys, I could not have accomplished this. I also thank my parents for their support and my brother for his encouragement.

Several friends have served as typists, sounding boards, and encouragers. Susan Springall, Suzanne Duffey, Judy Muffley, Joyce Trussell, and Yolanda Griswold have been such great encouragers and supporters in prayer. Thanks also to Kris Adair and Althea Parker for their encouraging notes that became part of this text.

My church family and pastors at McGehee

Road Baptist Church offered much support and validation. Thanks to Rev. Neal Hughes and Mrs. Carolyn Swafford who provided assistance in proofreading.

A special thanks also goes to Fred Springall for all his help.

PART I

BE FAITHFUL
TO YOUR CALLING

SHHH!
THE TEACHER'S COMING!

Read: John 10:1–6

When he has brought out all his own,
he goes on ahead of them,
and his sheep follow him
because they know his voice.
JOHN 10:4

Sometimes Coach Boyd would remain in the hall outside our government class for a few minutes after the bell rang. Almost on cue, one of the boys in the class would step to the door and announce, "Hey, Coach! They need you in the office." Since our classroom was on the far side of the building on the top floor, and the high school office was centrally located downstairs, this trick usually allowed us at least five minutes to socialize. When we heard Coach huffing and puffing back up the stairs, we opened our books and got quiet.

Like Coach Boyd, when someone calls your name, do you turn quickly to see who it is? (Note that I said "name"; I don't generally respond to "Hey, you!") Most of us want to be called by name —and that is how God calls us. Our shepherd, who knows us individually, takes pleasure in calling us by name. We are His flock, His children, whom He loves and gave His life to save. We are precious to Him.

When God calls us, He will lead if we are willing to follow. He will direct our paths and prepare the way by affording opportunities that help us recognize and develop our talents and gifts. Have you ever played "Follow the Leader" with the leader at the end of the line? Of course not! A leader steps out in front, and so does our good shepherd. He will be there so we can see the way to go.

To follow Jesus—to respond to His call—we must first get still and learn to listen for His voice. How do you start? By prayer, your wireless communication tool. Just as you use a telephone to talk and listen, when you pray, you do likewise. Many times I have been guilty of going to God with a string of questions, complaints, and requests and doing all the talking. Then I have hung up on God before I could even listen for His voice.

Second, we must keep our spiritual eyes open to see where He leads. Our physical sight has nothing to do with our ability to follow the shepherd. I have some visually impaired friends whose spiritual vision is 20/20. They have seen God's plan clearly and followed His calling. We must be careful to avoid the things of the world that will cloud our vision.

Finally, we must remember that God deals with us directly. God will neither force His way into our hearts nor will He play mind games with us. God is not the author of confusion. Unlike Satan, who sneaks in the "back door" of our hearts to surprise, steal, and destroy, God enters only by the "front door," or the main entrance.

The Lord says to us, "Here I am! I stand at the door and knock. If anyone hears my voice and opens the door, I will come in and eat with him, and he with me" (Revelation 3:20). If you recognize the shepherd of your heart's voice, let Him in now.

Heavenly Father, thank You for being the shepherd of my heart. Thank You for living in me, calling me, and leading me in Your ways. Forgive me when I fail to listen to Your voice. Amen.

WHOSE WILL?

Read: Philippians 2:12–18

*For it is God who works in you to will
and to act according to his good purpose.*
PHILIPPIANS 2:13

What motivated you to become a teacher? What motivates and inspires you to serve as a volunteer in your church, school, or community? According to this passage, our motivation should be from God. If we allow God to work in us, He will guide us to serve according to His divine purpose.

So often I have found myself ill at ease and without peace because I was not in God's will. That dissatisfaction spread like poison ivy; I was irritable, and nothing seemed to satisfy me. The only thing that could restore my peace and joy was to get aligned with the Lord's will. This revelation soon helped me devise my "standard" for knowing when I am centered in God's will—and that is when I experience the "peace that passes understanding" (see Philippians 4:7).

One's motivation for teaching may come from many sources, but for the Christian it should be a sense of calling. As teachers, we do far more than dispense information. I consider the noncurricular teaching more important than the curricular because I am giving children tools for living in society. Teaching respect for self and others, conflict resolution, and basic manners prepare children for life.

Many students come to school without these skills or a role model in the home environment. Maybe God has given you a particularly challenging student because He wants you to make a difference in that child's life. The results are not always immediately noticeable, but you have planted the seeds.

One particularly hyperactive and disruptive boy tried very hard to make me dislike him. It was a challenge, but I kept finding little things I could praise him for daily. Slowly the mask disappeared, and there was a child who desperately needed to be loved unconditionally. Years later, this boy called to invite me to his baptism. What a joy to see this boy maturing and trusting in his heavenly Father! Maybe a seed I had planted in second grade had sprouted.

Lord, I know You have called me to this career. Please renew my sense of calling and help me to stay true to Your will. Use me to reach students by showing them Your love each day. Amen.

SUCCESS 101

Read: 1 Thessalonians 2:1–11

You know, brothers,
that our visit to you was not a failure. . . .
For you know that we dealt with each of
you as a father deals with his own children,
encouraging, comforting and urging you
to live lives worthy of God,
who calls you into his kingdom and glory.
1 THESSALONIANS 2:1, 11–12

Are you a success story?

Did you make a difference today?

Did you leave your mark and make the world a better place?

No, you say.

Well, let's take a closer look.

Beyond the textbooks and work sheets,
Beyond the biology lab and field trip,
I'll bet you made a difference.

What about Jonetta? Didn't you encourage her to try the math problems again and help align her problems? She got it on the second try because you encouraged her.

And Bob—the little boy whose puppy was hit by a car? Didn't you put a gentle hand on his shoulder and offer him some tissues? Didn't you invite him to sit by you at lunch so he could talk about his puppy?

Oh, yes, what about Bailey and Edward? You know, those two rascals who were trying to fight before school? You took them to the office, but you stopped along the way to counsel them peacefully.

And then, there's the new teacher on your hall, Miss Lee. Didn't you offer to help her get her room set up? You even offered to let her use some of your materials until she could get on her feet. You even explained the daily procedures to her.

Yes, I thought so. You did make a difference. You are a success!

THE MEASURE OF SUCCESS

Read: Micah 6:6–8

He has showed you, O man, what is good.
And what does the LORD require of you?
To act justly and to love mercy
and to walk humbly with your God.
MICAH 6:8

As I have grown in my faith and developed a deeper relationship with God, I have come to understand that God places us in specific situations for a reason. To be sensitive and obedient to the divine plan is a tremendous joy.

There have been years, especially when I was burned out, when I really wondered why I was still teaching at the same school. But every time I have wondered, God has shown me someone that needed me to share His love. To touch one life adds a new dimension to the joy of living.

In a time when Christian teachers seem particularly wary of expressing their faith at school, I encourage you to reach out beyond your comfort zone to touch lives and minister with grace and compassion. You don't have to preach in your classroom. Consider some of these opportunities to be a witness for our Lord.

Whenever tensions are running high in your classroom, close the textbooks and talk about real life. Students need to hear about the Golden Rule and about personal accountability for their choices. This is true of every age group. Some of these children are products of hostile, negative environments where they are not taught these values. They have not heard that one must be a friend to have a friend.

Be sensitive to that student who needs some individual guidance and encouragement. Perhaps he is under tremendous peer pressure to behave contrary to his values. Maybe his mother has been diagnosed with cancer, or a close friend has been killed. Your sensitivity and words of encouragement may make the difference in the path he chooses to follow.

Be an encourager to the parents. Encourage a struggling single parent to return to school to get her GED or college degree. Supply parents with resources, articles, and common-sense advice to help them help their children. I give parents copies of Dr. James Dobson's newspaper columns and copies of pertinent magazine articles. If they have Internet access, I even recommend good Web sites.

Offer physical assistance when you see a need. Always ask the parents if they will accept the hand-me-downs before you dispense them. Respect their pride if they refuse your offer. The compassionate gesture in itself speaks volumes.

Don't be shy about telling parents or students that you will pray for them and their families, especially in times of crisis. I send a letter to parents at the beginning of school telling them what they can expect from me regarding discipline, homework, and so on. I ask the parents to pray for me throughout the year, and I tell them I will be praying for their families. This has opened many doors for me to minister to students and their families. Parents will drop in to tell me of a family member's illness or death and ask me to pray.

Look for opportunities to pray for someone at

school. One of mine has been a personal ministry to a struggling coworker whom the Lord placed on my heart. I began praying for her several months before she confided in me. From this prayer relationship emerged a very special friendship and partnership. Seeing her grow in faith has been thrilling.

Be sensitive to those teachable moments and experiences that can create new bonds between people. When the Challenger space shuttle exploded before our eyes on television in 1986, the event stunned my class. A fragmented group of children who had previously been emotionless and distant bonded in this new experience of grief. Students who had seemed apathetic and cynical requested and helped plan a simple but meaningful memorial service to honor the crew members. Being open to their ideas and sensitive to their feelings allowed a kinder and more caring side of them to be revealed.

When you reach a point where you can honestly pray this prayer, be ready for God to answer in some very special ways. Then put action with the prayers.

Dear Lord, I submit myself to You to be Your agent of change in my world. Help me to be sensitive to the needs of those around me and ready to respond and minister in Your love. Sometimes I wonder what I am doing here, but I trust You to show me my purpose here and beyond the chalk dust and textbooks. I lay myself upon the altar and simply say, "Whatever, Lord, may Thy will be done." Amen.

IN GOOD COMPANY

Read: Proverbs 13:14–20

He who walks with the wise grows wise,
but a companion of fools suffers harm.
PROVERBS 13:20

"You are known by the company you keep." Many of us were raised hearing this adage, and now we stress this truth to our own children. Although my dearest friends through the years have come from varied backgrounds, the cement that holds my relationship with them together is our common faith in Jesus Christ.

What kind of company do we keep in our professional lives? Do we seek the guidance of those teachers who have poor reputations? Not likely. We want to learn from the masters. When

I needed advice about classroom discipline, I turned to Margaret, a teacher who never seemed to get her feathers ruffled. When I needed some fresh ideas, I consulted Jane, the most creative teacher on campus.

Similarly, we should seek the company and advice of others who will encourage us in our walk of faith. This is not to say that we should shun nonbelievers. How can we be witnesses if we never have contact with those who need to know about Jesus? As we are watching and emulating others, someone may be watching us as role models. Hopefully, our positive influence will in turn make that person a role model for another.

After twenty-five years of teaching, my greatest joys have occurred when students, parents, and coworkers thank me for some bit of encouragement I offered them. Let's lift each other up so the world won't tear us down.

Lord, I have been so blessed with encouraging and inspiring friendships and professional acquaintances. Use me, Lord, to be a positive influence. Open my eyes to the person who needs my encouragement this day. Amen.

A TEACHER'S PRAYER

Read: Colossians 3:22–24

Whatever you do,
work at it with all your heart,
as working for the Lord, not for men.
COLOSSIANS 3:23

Lord, I think if I hear one more child tattling, I will scream!

Whatever you do, work at it with all your heart.

Lord, I am so burned out and stressed out! I need a break or another career!

Whatever you do, work at it with all your heart.

Lord, I know You know my heart. I love the children but hate all the paperwork. I hate collecting money for one thing and then another! I just want to teach!

Whatever you do, work at it with all your heart.

God, I just want to close my classroom door and teach without any interruptions for one whole day! Every time I turn around, someone is coming in asking a question, or the office is calling me on the intercom.

Whatever you do, work at it with all your heart.

You know, Lord, there are just too many things to remember to do each day! How can I get it all done and still have a life with my family?

Whatever you do, work at it with all your heart.

Sometimes I feel like I'm just talking to the walls. Does anyone care that I am even here? What does it matter?

Whatever you do, work at it with all your heart,

as working for the Lord, not for men.
COLOSSIANS 3:23

*Thank You, Lord. I know You care what
happens to me. I know this is my calling,
and that my reward will come later. I will
serve with enthusiasm and excellence. Accept
my work as my offering unto You. Amen.*

SUPPORT YOUR ADMINISTRATION

Read: 1 Timothy 6:1–6

*All who are under the yoke of slavery
should consider their masters
worthy of full respect,
so that God's name and our teaching
may not be slandered.
Those who have believing masters
are not to show less respect for them
because they are brothers.
Instead, they are to serve them even better,
because those who benefit from their service
are believers, and dear to them.
These are the things you are to teach
and urge on them.*
1 TIMOTHY 6:1–2

I consider myself to have been extraordinarily blessed during my career. It has been my joy and privilege to work with some of the finest and most caring administrators, several of whom are strong Christians.

Each principal has possessed unique strengths that filled specific needs at the time for our school. Each one has exercised a unique leadership style. Some of these styles have been very relaxed, while others have been more decisive and direct. Some have had an open-door policy, inviting the staff to come in anytime we needed to talk. With some I have shared prayer concerns, while others have been more guarded and less involved in the personal lives of staff members.

I have not always agreed with the administrators. Differences of opinion regarding student discipline, curriculum, grading policies, and other issues have surfaced. Some issues have been emotional flash points. My passion-driven motives have met resistance in the front office. There have been times when we were required to perform extra duties that were unpleasant or burdensome.

In those times of disagreement, it has been so easy to succumb to temptation. Negative comments have easily been directed toward the principal rather than the situation, and a nasty cycle of complaints, denials, and blaming has followed. Disagreements have taken on a far too personal nature, and grudge matches resulted. Human nature in all its imperfections was fully displayed. To say that I have always risen above such behavior would not be truthful.

However, I know that my rightful role as a teacher is to try to support my administrative staff. Regardless of my personal preferences, I am compelled by the grace of God to be an encourager and peacemaker in my workplace. If I truly believe God called me to teach in this school, then I must also believe He expects me to be a beacon of light there. I may not agree in theory or principle with all my administrators ask of me, but I can disagree respectfully and privately and then move on. I can and must support these leaders through prayer. I can give encouragement with special words of thanks when I am allowed to leave early for an appointment, or offer a word of genuine praise for a specific cause.

Someone said that life is 10 percent what happens to you, and 90 percent how you respond. I believe my response to school leadership is the determining factor in whether I have a successful day, week, or year.

Lord, thank You for the leaders of our schools. Give them wisdom and strength of character. Help us to be encouragers to these leaders. Make us sensitive to their needs. Amen.

A PRINCIPAL'S PRAYER

Lord, You have ordained the need for wise counsel and leadership.

You have placed me in this position of authority and responsibility.

The weight of the responsibility is daunting at times. I feel crushed beneath this load.

I need Your wisdom, Father, as I lead my staff. Help me to stand for truth and not be swayed by popular opinion. Help me be a positive example to my staff.

Lord, give me words of wisdom, grace, and

strength when my adversaries attack me. Help me treat the most irate parent with the same respect I would give an honored guest.

But also give me the strength of character to stand firm in my convictions.

Give me the physical and mental strength I need to face each day's challenges. Open my eyes to see the blessings of each day, too.

Thank You for this opportunity to lead.

Amen.

A LESSON FROM LEAVES

Read: Psalm 24:1–6

The earth is the LORD's,
and everything in it,
the world, and all who live in it.
PSALM 24:1

As I sit by the window overlooking our backyard, I notice the leaves are already falling. A summer drought has caused the leaves to drop prematurely. Watching the leaves reminds me of students.

Some leaves flutter about softly, gracefully, and gently, as if they are in no particular hurry. Like Amy and Michael, they have a quiet beauty and serenity. Other leaves seem to plummet head-on toward certain demise. They are driven and intense like Rob and Lashundra. Still others seem to drift slowly and aimlessly, driven by the shifts in the wind, much like Kenya and Allison. They, too, are easily influenced. Then there are the frenetic twirlers that seem compulsively driven and stay in constant motion. These are the Willies, Ashtons, and Johns.

The leaves create a kaleidoscope of colors and shapes as they are strewn across the lawn. Some are brilliant reds, yellows, and oranges, while others are nondescript shades. The sizes and shapes are as varied as the colors. Some are delicate, and others are thick, palm-sized fans. Even though the leaves are different, they seem randomly to collect into piles, much like children congregating on the playground. Yes, there are even some loners who seem content to linger along the borders.

As I look at the leaves, I can see the mess they create in my yard and the work that needs to be done. However, I choose to see them, at least for the moment, as a magnificent tapestry woven by the creator. I can see my students in the same way. I can celebrate each child's unique personality and strengths or complain about his weaknesses and how much work there is to be done.

The psalmist said that the world and the

people in it are all God's creation. With this in mind, let's try to celebrate the diversity and uniqueness of our students who weave a distinctive tapestry each year.

～

Thank You, God, for Your creation. Thank You for the uniqueness of each of us. Help me to see my students through heaven's eyes and to see the beauty in each child in his or her diversity. Amen.

A PRAYER FOR
MY STUDENTS

Heavenly Father, I praise Your name and Your
marvelous creation. As the psalmist said, everything
in the world belongs to You. I thank You for Your
most special creation—humankind.

Lord, I know that You have created each of us in
Your own image. Every one of us is precious to You.
Help me, Lord, to value each child in my class as
You do.

Lord, I can't change the world. I can't fix all the
problems my students bring to school. But with Your
help, I can touch each one in some way and let them
know they are persons of worth.

Father, I confess that my patience is often so short
with my students. I may brush them aside in the guise
of being too busy to listen. Sometimes I do not hear

what the children say. Sometimes it is easier to close my eyes and ears and not know the burdens they bring and the horrors they have seen.

Please forgive my impatience and indifference. Help me to get to know each student and understand his or her needs. Give me wisdom to know how You would have me respond as Your agent of love, mercy, and encouragement here on earth. Help me to see the children through Your eyes.

Thank You for every child entering my classroom today. Protect them and bless them. In Your most holy name, I pray.

Amen.

THOSE DAILY PLANS

Read: Proverbs 16:1–7

Commit to the LORD
whatever you do,
and your plans will succeed.
PROVERBS 16:3

"Good morning, class! Today we have a special activity. In the story we read yesterday—"

"Excuse me, Mrs. Robinson, we need you in the office," blares the intercom.

"Class, open your books to page 98 and read silently. I will be right back."

"Now, as I was saying, in the story we read yester-day the setting was long ago in the 1800s. What were some ways that they celebrated holidays back then that are different from how you celebrate today?"

"Mrs. Robinson, tell Raphael to give me my pencil!"

"I don't have your pencil, Girl!"

"Beth, I will clear up this matter with you and Raphael later. Now, how did the story's characters celebrate Christmas?"

"Teachers, please excuse this interruption. We will have a severe weather drill in a few minutes. Please take a moment to review the procedures with your students."

Have you ever had a really exciting lesson planned, only to have it foiled by constant interruptions? Isn't this frustrating? There was a time when such distractions would spoil my entire day. I went home irritable because the day had not gone according to *my* plans. Then it occurred to me one day that *my* plans are not of eternal consequence; *my* plans are not that important in the scheme of the universe.

To relieve yourself from this stress and frustration, think of your plans as a road map. You can see where you are headed, and you have a preferred route mapped out. Along the way there will inevitably be construction delays, detours, and some unplanned events. How you handle the unexpected will largely determine how your students learn to manage change. You may not accomplish a goal until tomorrow or next week, but you have some unique learning opportunities to teach some bonus lessons about life.

When your plans are thwarted, don't despair. Look for the silver lining and the hidden lessons this temporary delay may offer. If you commit your plans to the Lord, you will succeed in God's way and in His time frame.

*Lord, help me as I plan the lessons for my
students. Help me plan with care and to
remember these are only ideas on paper.
When things don't go my way, help me to see
the situation through Your eyes. Help me to
make the best of each day and to remember
it is a gift from You. Amen.*

A CONCUSSION

Read: Proverbs 4:20–27

Let your eyes look straight ahead,
fix your gaze directly before you.
Make level paths for your feet
and take only ways that are firm.
Do not swerve to the right or the left;
keep your foot from evil.
PROVERBS 4:25–27

Recently, in one of my more graceful moments, I butted my head into a wall. (I'm exaggerating slightly.) Actually, I tripped over a rug and fell headfirst into a bookcase full of picture frames and figurines. In an effort not to break any items, I managed to shift my body and hit the wall.

The next day I felt like a sailor on rough seas. The walls were tilting about thirty degrees and I found myself walking into walls and stumbling. A visit to the doctor revealed that I had suffered a concussion. I was ordered to bed to rest until I was more surefooted, and my vision was clearer.

Reflecting on this event, I realized that I have had a spiritual concussion before. The causes have been varied. I was immature and allowed false doctrines to cloud my mind. There were times when I didn't want to listen to God's call. I disobeyed or ignored my heavenly Father. There have been periods of anger and rebellion when I felt God was not listening to my prayers or was too slow answering. There was a period of depression when I couldn't think straight. In each case, I stumbled into a spiritual abyss. I lost my focus on the author and perfecter of my faith.

The good news is that God's loving hand always rescued me and set my feet on firm ground again. Slowly I am learning to trust God for whatever comes my way. I have to keep looking ahead at the glorious finish line and stay on a straight course. When I pray, "Lead us not into temptation," I understand that I have a responsibility not to allow myself to be misled. In keeping a straight path, I hope that I will also be a worthy guide for someone else, to help keep her feet planted on firm ground.

That is when I know I am on the solid ground that is level at the foot of Calvary.

Dear Lord, please forgive me when I allow myself to be led in the evil ways of the world. Help me to keep my focus on You and Your way of righteousness. Thank You, Lord, for rescuing me and leading me back to Your will each time I stray. Amen.

HOW'S YOUR VISION?

Read: Proverbs 29:18; Hebrews 11:1, 6

*Now faith is being sure of what we hope for
and certain of what we do not see.*
HEBREWS 11:1

One of my favorite inspirational speakers and authors is Luci Swindoll. Luci's definitions of faith and vision really strike a chord with me. She says that vision is being able to see things in ways that others don't, and faith is being able to do things when others won't.

I wonder how many times I have limited God's power because of a lack of vision or faith. Sometimes I get so overwhelmed by the myriad of tasks that I need to complete that all I can see is the mountain of work before me. Public distrust, lack of parental support, inconsistent support from superiors, and ever-changing special education regulations seem to limit my vision. I feel like I am looking at life through a knothole and can only see a small portion from that vantage point. I can list all the problems readily, but the solutions are not forthcoming. I do have some good ideas, but I find that I am waiting for someone else to be likewise inspired and carry them to completion.

Public education in America is at a crossroads. I don't believe the heart of the problem is a lack of vision. There are many talented, creative, and visionary professionals in our schools. I know there are viable solutions for local problems just lying dormant, much like a slumbering giant.

What our profession seems to lack is faith— faith in our own abilities, in our communities, in our leadership. But underlying that is a lack of faith that God will do what He said He will. Our mistrust in a problem-riddled system has given way to our limiting God's power. If we really trust God to be omnipotent, then we must give life to our visions. We must rise to give heart to the ideas burning within us. We must be willing to step across the threshold of our comfort zones into uncharted territories to put feet to our faith.

I am at a juncture in my professional life and my faith. I feel God is leading me into new territory. I have a vision of what He has planned for me. Will I perish because I let the vision die, or will I prosper by stepping out in faith?

Has God given you a vision? Is God calling you to step to the forefront and lead the charge in the new millenium? What will be your response?

Dear God, I yield myself to Your calling. I must allow You to be God, to be the Master of my life, and to allow Your power and glory to be fully displayed. Forgive me for my lack of faith. Help me be more faithful. Amen.

THANKS FOR THE MEMORIES

Read: Phillippians 1:3–7

I thank my God every time I remember you.
PHILIPPIANS 1:3

Trimming the Christmas tree has become a very sentimental affair in our home, thanks to my many students. Over the years they have bestowed upon me an eclectic menagerie of ornaments as Christmas gifts. Each ornament has been carefully labeled, and as I unwrap them, memories flood my mind.

The lovely dove is from a gentle, peaceful girl who was searching for her identity. That brass ornament reflects the Christmas lights with a warmth seen in the eyes of another young girl of bygone days. The angel made of baby socks reminds me of a kind and helpful parent of a dear student.

There is a miniature wooden car given by a thoughtful boy who thought my toddler would like it. The carousel horse is from a student who struggled with a speech impediment but articulated his affection eloquently in kind deeds.

Some of the ornaments are less attractive but oh, so dear. The clothespin reindeer was made by a student who lacked the means to purchase a gift. The bottle-cork horse was made by another who said his mother always threw away his crafts. The candy canes were projects made in Girl Scouts by a lovely girl years ago.

A beautiful decoupage ball was presented by a sixth-grade girl who had only shown contempt for me in class. With it was a handwritten card expressing thanks for my discipline and guidance. One of the seemingly gruff and tough guys in my sixth-grade class selected and wrapped two exquisite ceramic musical instrument ornaments. He said he liked harp and trumpet music, and he wanted me to remember him that way.

Yes, every ornament seems to tell a story that has been etched on my heart. When the frustrations of teaching have made my work seem so futile, these precious trinkets have validated my efforts. If I have reached one child during a single year, my efforts have not been in vain.

Thank You, Lord, for each child who has touched my life. Thanks for the memories of special people. Bless each giver with peace, love, and joy. Amen.

PART II

MAKE A DIFFERENCE

THE MASTER TEACHER

Read: Job 36:22–26; Matthew 13:3–15

God is exalted in his power.
Who is a teacher like him?
JOB 36:22

Jesus' ministry was a display of unequalled teaching. A man without a college education impacted the world two thousand years ago and continues to do so today through His words recorded in the Holy Bible. Jesus was the Master; He was also a master teacher. And there are three keys to His effectiveness that I think we can apply to our personal and professional lives.

First, Jesus was real. He was a living, breathing, walking, talking man with whom people could communicate. He had needs. He had feelings. He got angry and impatient with certain people. He felt anguish, sorrow, and joy, and He shared these with His disciples.

In my class each year, there are always a few students who are amazed to learn that I have a life away from school. I keep a photo cube on my desk so they can see my family, including my dog. I share with them things I do in my spare time (church, hobbies, trips). I also tell them when I am worried about something. When students know I am real, often they will come and share concerns with me.

Jesus was also relevant. Relevance is important in effective teaching since it gives the learner a reason to listen. To accomplish this, Jesus used parables, or vivid lessons that illustrated spiritual concepts with everyday objects, to teach most of His truths. Whether it was a fig tree, a vine, or a house built on sand, Jesus used animate and inanimate objects from His surroundings to illustrate a truth and make it understandable. Likewise, we can be resourceful in our efforts to teach the curriculum and to enrich our students' lives. Be creative in thinking of ways to share your faith with people, too.

Jesus was the perfect role model. He didn't just tell people how to live; He showed them every minute of His life. Educators are being asked to teach character education and values that were once taught by parents. Some of our students' homes are devoid of any positive role models. You can be a godly role model and demonstrate the values you teach each day. Model appropriate speech, self-control, ethics, and interpersonal relationships in your school and community. For me, the hardest place to be the consistent role model is at home where I can be myself. Sometimes the real me isn't as positive as I need to be.

If Jesus were walking the earth today, He would be a nominee for every award available. However, Jesus never sought acclaim. He was just busy doing His Father's will. Our challenge is to imitate Christ daily in our workplace and community.

Lord, help me to follow Your example by being real and relevant to my students each day. Help me to be a good role model for them. Thank You for being the perfect role model for teachers. Amen.

A MODEL OF
SELF-CONTROL

Read: 2 Timothy 2:23–26

Don't have anything to do with
foolish and stupid arguments,
because you know they produce quarrels.
And the Lord's servant must not quarrel;
instead, he must be kind to everyone,
able to teach, not resentful.
2 TIMOTHY 2:23–24

As I approached the end of a twenty-five-year career in teaching, people often asked me how education has most changed in the past quarter of a century. Certainly teaching methods, technology, and increased emphasis on individualization have effected positive changes. Multiculturalism and humanism have also impacted schools. However, the biggest difference I have noticed is the effect of the moral breakdown of our culture and the lack of respect for authority that breakdown has generated.

When I was a child, I would never have dreamed of arguing with a teacher or any other adult. To argue with an adult was disrespectful and would have resulted in swift and certain punishment. Today children are allowed to argue, plead, and bargain with their parents, and the same behavior is considered appropriate in school. How should we as Christian educators respond? I can only speak from personal experience and observation. I would not pretend to be an authority on this subject.

One of my son's favorite elementary schoolteachers continues to be a beautiful example of this verse in action. Margaret is the most loving and nurturing teacher a parent could desire. Her class is also the most orderly. There students learn to follow directions and respect authority. They learn self-control, self-respect, and accountability for their choices.

Margaret is a woman of few words but a great role model for the children to emulate. In eighteen years I have never heard her raise her voice, nor have I seen her negotiate with a child. She is the epitome of patience. When she gives directions, she quietly waits until every child complies. She does not tolerate children arguing with her, and yet she is always fair.

Likewise, I have never seen Margaret publicly argue with a parent or another teacher. Her discretion and mild manner have earned her the respect of many. When she disagrees, she does so quietly, calmly, respectfully, and privately. Even in the face of harsh criticism doled out by irate parents in full view of others, this woman exhibits self-control and stands firm in her convictions. Often those same parents are the ones who are singing her praises loudest by year's end.

Because Margaret not only demands respect but also treats others with respect, her classes have produced some very high achievers. Her secret to success is her relationship with the Lord Jesus Christ and her willingness to follow His example and teachings.

Lord, thank You for Margaret and the many other educators who are such a positive influence in our schools. Shape me and mold me to be more self-disciplined. Help me live the Golden Rule daily as an example for my students. Amen.

WORDS OF GRACE

Read: Colossians 4:5–6;
Proverbs 15:1

A gentle answer turns away wrath,
but a harsh word stirs up anger.
PROVERBS 15:1

As I walked down the hall at school, I heard some-one screaming and cursing. Turning the corner, I encountered a parent and teacher confrontation. The parent was cursing the teacher, and the teacher was exhibiting remarkable self-control by not retaliating.

The parent passed me in the hall a few min-utes later, gloating after her vicious attack. Quietly I asked, "Aren't you the one who gives testimony in the church TV commercial?" She basked in the recognition for a moment. Then I said, "Is this the way God calls you to treat people?" Her reply stunned me. "God didn't call me to be a sissy or a doormat. I was just standing up for my son." I turned away in disbelief.

The apostle Paul wrote that our words are to be "full of grace, seasoned with salt" (Colossians 4:6), and in Matthew 5:13 Jesus Himself said that we are "the salt of the earth." Salt adds a distinctive flavor to foods, and it is also a preservative. Our words should set us apart from nonbelievers and preserve our witness. We can speak courteously to people when we are angry. The manner in which we speak should say as much about our witness as our words. Sometimes saying nothing and simply walking away is most effective.

Pray for God's grace to permeate and season your speech so that you can be a faithful witness as you respond to criticism. Before conferences, pray for God to give you a right spirit and just the right words of grace to say. You will be amazed at the results.

Lord, give me gracious words when I

respond to criticism. Give me insight and understanding to be able to address parents' concerns. Give me a humble spirit. May my words be pleasing to You. Amen.

BEING A POINT OF LIGHT

Read: 2 Corinthians 4:6;
Matthew 5:14–16

For God, who said,
"Let light shine out of darkness,"
made his light shine in our hearts
to give us the light of the knowledge
of the glory of God in the face of Christ.
2 CORINTHIANS 4:6

When George Bush was campaigning for president in 1988, he issued a challenge to Americans to become "a thousand points of light." Almost two thousand years before, our Lord and Savior Jesus Christ issued a similar challenge to His followers.

How can we continually be those points of

light that glorify God? Here is a laundry list of ideas:

- Open doors for the elderly, the handicapped, and the encumbered.

- Call a shut-in and tell her she is in your prayers and thoughts.

- Commit one day of personal leave time to volunteer for a charitable organization.

- Visit an elderly or visually impaired person and offer to read or write letters for him.

- Take toys to a shelter for battered women and children.

- Take children's drawings to a nursing home or a children's ward in a hospital.

- Invite someone who has no local family to share a holiday meal with your family.

- Take a fresh bouquet of flowers or a basket of muffins to your doctor's office staff.

- Take a gallon of cold water or lemonade to a construction crew and say, "Have a nice day!"

- Offer to drive a disabled neighbor to the grocery store or doctor's office.

These are actions that can take as little as five seconds or as long as a day. The point is that once you have performed one kind action, it is easier to perform another. When you help someone else, it may well inspire him or her to help another. Kindness begets kindness.

Now can you take it a step further? Can you find ways to help your students become points of light? Find a project suitable for your students' age, interests, and abilities. A high school history class could visit a veterans' hospital and talk with war heroes for some firsthand research information. A middle-school class might create riddle cards to send to children in a hospital. Kindergarten students could visit a senior day-care center to sing.

Kindness is a characteristic that must be exercised to be developed. It is also a characteristic that needs to be cultivated through positive role models and opportunities. Be that role model for your students and that source of inspiration to others. Be the one who will find the time to be a light in the darkness and be a blessing to someone else.

Lord, help me be sensitive to ways that I can shine for You and point others to Your light. Amen.

M.Y.O.B

Read: Romans 14:13–19

*Therefore let us stop passing judgment
on one another.
Instead, make up your mind
not to put any stumbling block or obstacle
in your brother's way.*
ROMANS 14:13

Why is it that some people seem to make minding others' business their mission in life? Perhaps you know someone who is constantly snooping and gossiping. Or maybe you know people who are always checking on each other's plans and competing to be the best and showiest, as though the one with the most projects wins a prize.

Some people seem to take great pleasure in judging others—and measuring them against their own "perfect" standard. If they kept these assessments to themselves, everyone would fare better. By broadcasting their critiques, not only do they fan flames of resentment among peers, but they set a poor example for children. Is it any wonder that children put one another down so freely?

The gossipmongers are always on the prowl for a juicy bit of truth that can be stretched and sensationalized, and every school staff seems to have at least two. It's hard to gossip without an accomplice. Early in my career I made the grave mistake of listening to a gossip's tale about someone having an adulterous relationship. Had I just listened and kept my mouth shut, I could have avoided an embarrassing situation for all of us. However, I repeated this juicy story to a colleague who promptly told the subjects of this fabrication. To my embarrassment, I was confronted by these individuals. It was inexcusable, and to have said, "But *she* told me!" would not have mattered. I had to eat my words, and they were not pleasant. What's more, I had to ask these people for forgiveness. I almost destroyed my credibility with them.

When I am tempted to pry, I remember this

Chinese proverb: The man who minds his neighbor's business cannot keep his own shop. Let me point out that this does not imply we are islands, isolated from one another. We need that interdependence in our schools to build a sense of community that allows us to work as a team toward common goals. We need to care for one another and bear one another's burdens at times. This is a privilege not to be abused by wagging tongues when our colleagues have placed their personal trust and confidence in us.

We can help the present generation of children learn what community and caring are about from God's standard when we set the example. Perhaps your classroom's rules can include standards for personal accountability and showing kindness to others in word and deed. Then we will all be elevated to a higher plane and honor God.

Lord, help me to guard my tongue that my words may be kind and set a godly example for my students and peers. Help me show sensitivity to others by not repeating confidential information. Amen.

STICKS AND STONES

Read: James 3:1–6

*Likewise the tongue is
a small part of the body,
but it makes great boasts.
Consider what a great forest is
set on fire by a small spark.*
JAMES 3:5

"Sticks and stones may break my bones, but words can never hurt me." We all learned this chant as children to defend ourselves when people teased us or called us names. Of course, truthfully, words can and do hurt us.

Several years ago I, was experiencing a most challenging class of sixth graders—and I was on the brink of a nervous breakdown. The combination of sixth-grade hormones and my premenopausal hormones just clashed at every turn! Talk about a wild, emotional roller coaster!

On several occasions, I had to pull my big foot out of my mouth and apologize to students. What was I thinking? Or was I even thinking? I allowed my frustrations to boil over and spew forth in venomous words. These were twelve-year-old children. I would never want anyone to speak to my child in this manner. I even called some parents to apologize for my tirades because their children had been innocent victims.

The part that troubled me most was not the unprofessional manner in which I handled situations, but that I had destroyed my witness and betrayed my Lord with my mouth. None of the excuses or reasons I used to rationalize my behavior would hold water.

I share this confession for two reasons. First, I would not be so presumptuous as to try to present myself as someone who has done it all right. Also, I want to encourage you to tame your tongues. Let your words be kind and full of love, especially toward your students. I urge you to let them see and feel the heavenly Father's love through you and your words. Let your words be your daily testimony of a loving God.

~

*Dear Father, I know You have forgiven me
for failing to control my tongue. Give me a
spirit of self-control and let my words mirror Your unconditional love. Amen.*

THE POSITIVE ROLE MODEL

Read: Philippians 4:4–9

Let your gentleness be evident to all.
The Lord is near.
Do not be anxious about anything,
but in everything, by prayer and petition,
with thanksgiving,
present your requests to God.
And the peace of God,
which transcends all understanding,
will guard your hearts and
your minds in Christ Jesus.
PHILIPPIANS 4:5–7

Think back to a teacher who was an inspirational role model to you. What unique qualities were evident in that person's life? As I reminisce about some of my favorite teachers who inspired me to teach, I recall that each one was enthusiastic and excited about her work. Their lives were joyful, and they radiated love and joy in their work. Yes, they had bad days, but they still expressed joy in living and in teaching.

There was only one teacher with whom I developed a close enough relationship that I could ask about her spiritual life. Married to a lay minister, she had a personal relationship with God and a walk with Christ that displayed those qualities described in the preceding Scripture. What must one do to have this kind of peace? Paul listed four things: Rejoice, be gentle, pray, and don't be anxious. These actions yield the wonderful peace of God.

Why rejoice? Joyful people attract others like honey calling to bees. No one wants to be around a complainer, and frowning is not attractive either. If we want to be good witnesses, we need to be happy.

Gentleness is also a character trait that draws people in. It's a salve for the callousness of this world. While the world offers meanness, apathy, and selfishness, the gentle nature of Jesus Christ is in sharp contrast.

Paul also said to stop worrying. Worrying is like a rocking chair: It gives you something to do but doesn't get you anywhere. Instead of worrying, ask God to help you see what to do, whether that means waiting on His timing or taking action. Prayer is the key that unlocks the door to peace. God's peace is like a rest stop, an oasis in life's long, winding road. God's peace in your heart will enable you to endure the hard times with grace and dignity. It doesn't mean you won't have problems or conflicts, but it does mean you will be equipped to handle what comes your way with God's help.

Be a positive role model for your students and colleagues so that they may see a joyful life in progress and give thanks to God.

Dear Lord, thank You for those who have influenced my spiritual life so much. Help me to be a positive role model. Equip me with Your peace and strength to handle the curveballs that life throws me. Amen.

PASS THE SALT!

Read: Matthew 5:13–16

You are the salt of the earth.
But if the salt loses its saltiness,
how can it be made salty again?
It is no longer good for anything,
except to be thrown out
and trampled by men.
MATTHEW 5:13

Salt is such a simple substance, yet it makes such a difference. I don't know about you, but I don't think God intended for some foods to be eaten unsalted! Grits, corn on the cob, and fresh tomatoes cry out for salt. Salt has a distinct flavor that permeates foods.

Salt is also a preservative substance. I can remember my grandparents curing pork after the hogs were slaughtered. Salt was necessary in preserving and curing the meat.

Salt also has healing properties. Have you ever gargled with warm saltwater for a sore throat? Salts added to warm water make a soothing solution for soaking feet. Even the fragrance of salty ocean water has a relaxing effect.

Isn't it interesting that Jesus told His followers, "You are the salt of the earth"? Jesus wants us to be distinctive, preserving, and healing agents in the world. The message for Christian educators, then, is that we are challenged to be distinctive in our workplaces.

While human laws may prevent us from some expressions of our faith, our lives should be dramatically different from nonbelievers. We should be walking, talking, breathing lessons in character education every day. We should be busy preserving peace in our schools, helping bring people together to a common ground. We should preserve our religious freedom and heritage. We can be the soothing salts that help heal hurt feelings, encourage the down-and-out, and lift up fellow teachers and students in prayer. Then we can be distinctively different and season our schools with God's love.

Lord, let me be Your saltshaker today! Use me to season my home, my school, and my community with Your grace and goodness. Help me to stay fresh so that I may be a more uplifting and positive witness. Amen.

A HERITAGE OF FREEDOM

Read: John 8:31–36; Psalm 51:12

To the Jews who had believed him,
Jesus said, "If you hold to my teaching,
you are really my disciples.
Then you will know the truth,
and the truth will set you free."
JOHN 8:31–32

Having studied and taught history for many years, I knew the facts about America's fight for freedom and independence. I knew America had also been a key player in wars that helped preserve world peace and freedom in other countries. However, my appreciation for this freedom was not realized until I visited our nation's capital.

While touring the monuments in Washington, D.C., I was deeply moved as I read the inscriptions on the Lincoln Memorial and Jefferson Memorial. Our forefathers knew that freedom was costly but worth the struggle. The Arlington National Cemetery and the Vietnam Veterans' Memorial touched me deeply; so many lives were given in the fight for freedom.

As we teach children about their American heritage and the freedoms granted in the United States Constitution, let us not forget to stress the freedom to worship. Therein lies the truest sense of freedom humans can know. Jesus said that when we hold to His teachings we will know the truth and truly be free. And what were Jesus' teachings? He said to love one another. He said to obey the laws of Moses, or the Ten Commandments. Our nation's laws are founded on the laws God gave to Moses. If we live according to God's laws, then abiding by human laws should not be a problem.

I am well aware of the Supreme Court rulings against organized school prayer and the restrictions for displaying religious items such as the Ten Commandments in public places. However, since the Ten Commandments are part of world history and Judaism, and the Constitution is an historical document, could we at least lead our students to compare the two documents? Without infringing on anyone's rights, can't we stress the value and importance of our rights and freedom, including the right to our own religious beliefs? What greater part of our heritage can we offer to the future generations? We can at least point them in the right direction.

Father in heaven, thank You for our nation's heritage of freedom and faith. Thank You for my heritage of faith. Help me to stay grounded in Your Word and to trust in You, the giver of freedom from sin's tyranny. Help me to find ways to infuse Your truths into my teaching. Amen.

PART III

TRUST GOD

A PRAYER FOR HELP

Lord, help me!
I am so overwhelmed
    by responsibilities
    by commitments
    by the needs of my family
    by grief and disappointment.
Lord, You know all that I need to do.
    You see the work piled on my desk,
    my cluttered house and untended flower beds.
    You know the promises I have made and
        those depending upon me.
    You know the emotional, physical, and
        spiritual needs of my loved ones.
    You understand the tears I've shed and
        the sense of loss I feel.
Lord, I feel like hiding in a cave and
    shutting the world out.

I just want to escape from it all.
I feel so alone!
Yet, I hear You calling to me, "What are
  you doing here?"

*And in that same, still, small voice Elijah heard so
long ago, and that the disciples loved, I hear Your
reassuring promise:*

*"Peace I leave with you; my peace I give you. I
do not give to you as the world gives. Do not let
your hearts be troubled and do not be afraid"* (John
14:27).

I feel so powerless and useless, Lord.
I can't heal the sick.
I can't change people's minds and hearts.
I can't be everything to everyone.
Let me pull a blanket over my head
and shut out everything.

Again, I hear Your gentle voice calling me.

*"Be strong and courageous. Do not be afraid or
terrified because of them, for the* LORD *your God
goes with you; he will never leave you nor forsake
you"* (Deuteronomy 31:6).

All right, Lord, I'm coming out. I'm still not certain how all of this will work out, but I place my trust in You for You are the Lord God, the one on whom I can always depend. Give me a sense of peace, and help me to see those things which I must do first.

Help me face the day with a calm and courageous spirit, knowing You'll help me each step of the way. Amen.

DON'T PANIC! HELP IS NEAR!

Read: Psalm 121:2–8

The LORD will keep you from all harm—
he will watch over your life;
the LORD will watch over your coming
and going both now and forevermore.
PSALM 121:7–8

One of the most distressing signs of the times is the mentality that one can get whatever he desires through litigation. As a special education teacher, I was keenly aware of the importance of following procedural guidelines to the letter. Whether following the mandated curriculum, adhering to school system policies, or complying with education laws, we must be diligent to follow the guidelines.

Prior to my retirement, I discovered a major procedural violation that I had made on a student's special education file. At first I panicked, and then I felt nauseous. The possible ramifications for this could be costly, but the worst consequence was having to admit my error. It was a hard pill to swallow as I always had a reputation for being meticulous in these matters. I was also afraid that the student's parents might seek litigation.

As I worked through my panic and fear, I thought about my professional organization. Would they be able to help me if this matter went to court? Would that liability insurance be of any value? Would I lose the trust and respect of my colleagues? In the midst of the crisis, God's Word came to minister to me and calm my fears. He is the wonderful counselor, Prince of peace, and mighty fortress—and much more. Soon the panic was replaced with peace and a calm reassurance that God would show me the way to resolve the problem.

His way is best. If my life were a highway, the road signs might well read, "Yield to God," "Stop the Panic," and "One Way—His Way."

Lord, thank You for ministering to me through Your peace and strength. Thank You for reminding me that I must seek You first and trust in You. I confess my pride and ask for a more humble spirit and a more careful eye to details. Amen.

EXPERIENCE NOT REQUIRED

Read: Luke 8:22–25

"Where is your faith?" he asked his disciples.
In fear and amazement
they asked one another, "Who is this?
He commands even the winds and the
water, and they obey him."
LUKE 8:25

In my tenth year of teaching, a special education teacher from another school came to inform me about a new student who was to transfer to my self-contained learning disabilities class. She proceeded to paint a very troubling picture of a spoiled brat and an overbearing, verbally abusive, alcoholic mother. Immediately fearful, I assumed that the tranquility of my class would be severely threatened.

In the Scripture, Jesus' disciples were on calm waters until a storm blew in and their peaceful, moonlit excursion was suddenly in peril. Were these men all novice sailors? Of course not, but every one of them was afraid for his life. Clearly, they had not realized and recognized Jesus' authority and His ability to save the perishing.

Fear is usually considered a negative emotion, but fear can have positive effects, too. Fear can spur one into action and self-preservation. Fear can motivate one to change destructive habits, such as when the fear of dying from cancer motivates a person to stop smoking.

What do you fear? Do you fear for the safety or health of a loved one? Do you fear the loss of someone in your life? Perhaps you are afraid of losing your job. You may fear being evaluated by your supervisors. Fear of failure is a very prevalent fear in professional circles. Do you fear losing control?

The disciples had a legitimate fear, the fear of drowning. Are your fears realistic or unfounded? Will you face them on your own, handling things in your own way? Or will you cry out to God and ask Him to save you? There is no shame in being afraid. Even seasoned sailors get scared on rough seas. Just remember to call upon God to calm the waters for you.

As things turned out, my new student was an adorable little girl whose mother was rightfully concerned for her child's safety and future. A deep friendship and spiritual kinship was born of that relationship, made possible only because God heard my prayer for help.

Thank You, God, for being my protection and giving me a calm spirit. Help me to remember that You will protect me in the rough seas of life if I put my trust in You. Amen.

THE HEART OF THE STORM

The sky grows darker by the minute.
The wind is strong and lightning's in it.
As the sirens start their wail
And the howling winds assail
I know I need not fear
For my Lord is always near.

As a fury rages in my soul
And all around me grows so cold—
As my mind is so bombarded,
My heart is safely guarded.
The master has the key;
I know He's watching me.

At the darkest point of night
Into my heart He shines His light
Guiding me away from danger.
A calming voice, not of a stranger,
Beckons me to safer shore
Where I will fear no more.

Praise be to the LORD,
for he has heard my cry for mercy.
The LORD is my strength and my shield;
my heart trusts in him,
and I am helped.
PSALM 28:6–7

WEATHERING LIFE'S STORMS

Read: Mark 4:35–41; Psalm 91

If you make the Most High your dwelling—
even the LORD, who is my refuge—
then no harm will befall you,
no disaster will come near your tent.
For he will command his angels concerning
you to guard you in all your ways.
PSALM 91:9–11

One of my favorite contemporary Christian songs says, "When I think I'm going under, part the waters, Lord."* So often this has been my prayer in times of stress. If my only role in life were to serve God through teaching, I would probably be lulled into thinking that I could handle life on my own.

God calls us to wear many hats. As a spouse, marriage demands our attention and energy. Even in the most loving and compatible relationships, there will be occasional disagreements and tension. As a mother or father, parenting compounds the responsibilities and demands upon our time and resources. When you've been up all night with a colicky baby or a sick child, your strength is drained and your nerves are on edge. Years later, parenting a teenager who is struggling with the boundaries you've set can be an enormous challenge.

As we grow older, many of us have found ourselves defined as the "Sandwich Generation," caring for both our children and our aging parents. Whether your parents live in your home, in their own home, or in a health-care facility, there is a tremendous burden to care for them and see that their needs are met. My father has been homebound and dependent upon an oxygen concentrator for thirteen years. We have had so many occasions to sit in the hospital with Daddy, sometimes unsure if he would live another day. Grieving for thirteen years will surely leave one feeling powerless and depressed.

Our jobs require increasingly greater investments of our time, energy, talents, and other inner resources. Often we are surrogate parents for students who have no one to give them structure, love, and guidance. Many nonteaching duties compete for our time and attention, as well.

Look to the Savior for your peace in the midst of life's storms. Some storms will be squalls that pass through quickly. Others will be monsoons that come and stay awhile and wreak havoc in our lives. Trust the Lord to calm the seas and guard you with His angels. Trust Him to deliver you.

Lord, please take my burdens and give me relief. I ask not for an easy life, but for strength to weather the storms of life. Give me a tranquil spirit in the face of difficulties so that You may be glorified. Amen.

*From "Part the Waters, Lord,"
words and music by CHARLES F. BROWN,
Word Music, Inc., 1975.

SEPARATION ANXIETY

Read: Romans 8:31–39

*No, in all these things we are more than
conquerors through him who loved us.*
ROMANS 8:37

It's the first day of school. The teachers have prepared the classrooms with stimulating bulletin
boards, interest centers, and displays. They are
ready to greet the wide-eyed, fresh-faced youth
who will be under their tutelage for the next several months. As the bell rings, the children spill
into the halls searching for assigned room num-
bers and greeting their friends.

Above the excited din a woeful wail is heard.
Then another. Ah, yes! It is indeed the first day

of school, and some kindergarten students are experiencing pangs of separation anxiety. For some, this is their first time away from their mothers all day. Each of them wonders silently, *Will Mommy still love me at the end of the day? Will she remember to come pick me up after school?*

As Christians we sometimes allow our fears and sinfulness to create a spiritual form of separation anxiety. When the apostle Paul wrote his epistle to the Romans, he was well aware that the Christians in Rome faced many forms of persecution. Paul's words of reassurance to the Romans are still true for Christ's followers today.

What can separate us from the love of Christ? Can our personal problems—divorce, bankruptcy, chemical dependence, rebellious teenagers—keep us from God's love? Can physical or mental suffering negate God's love? Can gossip, false accusations, unfair treatment, or religious persecution prevent us from grasping God's love? Can hunger, poverty, or emotional need block God's blessings? Can exposure, vulnerability, or violence keep us from the love of Christ?

Paul's resounding *"no"* is very comforting to me. There is nothing so horrible or unbearable or humiliating that I cannot still experience God's love. Once I have chosen to accept God's grace and have committed myself to Him, I am the recipient of His everlasting, omnipotent love that covers me for eternity. With this in mind, I can face the future with confidence.

Lord, Your omnipotence is indescribable. I praise Your name. Thank You for Your love for me that endures forever regardless of what happens in my life. Amen.

HOPE FOR THE FUTURE

Read: Jeremiah 29:11–13

"For I know the plans I have for you,"
declares the LORD,
"plans to prosper you and not to harm you,
plans to give you hope and a future."
JEREMIAH 29:11

As I scanned the newspaper, my attention was drawn to the details of a gunman's rampage. Another article detailed the execution-style slayings of two innocent teenage girls. The morning news programs repeated the same tragic stories. Such senseless acts of violence have eroded the sense of security our schools once offered.

Even though I grew up during the years of

racial unrest and civil rights marches, I do not recall ever being afraid to go to school. Today, though, we have lockdown drills at school to try to prepare for hostile intruders. We teach children about "Stranger Danger" starting in preschool. Children are taught to drop to the ground when they are outdoors and hear a loud noise that might be a gunshot. I find this all very sad—a robbery of childhood innocence.

Yet even in these times of unpredictable violence, we can be assured that God is still here in our midst, and He has not abandoned His drawing board. God's plans for us will be accomplished if we trust in Him and seek to know His will. As educators, we have a responsibility to reassure students that God is still in control and that His plan for us includes salvation through trusting in Jesus. Through our Christian lifestyles and loving attitudes, we can help children claim God's promise for a hope and a future.

Thank You, God, for Your providence and sovereign will. Lord, help me find ways to offer hope for the children's future. Help me be a voice of reassurance and reason in this world gone mad. Amen.

A PRAYER FOR PROTECTION

God of mercy,

Evil has permeated this nation; innocent lives have been shattered and lost because of selfishness, sickness, and sin in human hearts.

Lord, You know the pain and anguish of losing a child to violence.

We ask for Your divine intervention to stop the madness.

Father, please give Your heavenly hosts charge to form a protective hedge around every school.

Give Your angels power to dispel the demons of hatred, selfishness, fear, and deceit from the schools.

Help us as Christian educators to speak boldly in defense of what is right and just.

Help us to find ways to express Your love

and hope to the children in times of such despair and seeming hopelessness.

Protect us, Lord, we pray.

Amen.

PART IV

PERSEVERE

A PRAYER FOR A DIFFICULT DAY

Lord, You are the mighty God of the universe, creator of all the earth.

You control the forces of nature and have performed signs and miracles throughout the ages. I praise You for Your mighty power.

Lord, I am feeling so drained today. Things have not gone as I had planned. I am tired and frustrated; my mental, physical, emotional, and spiritual reserves are running low.

I am not sure if I can go on.

Lord, refill my cup and let me overflow with Your refreshing Spirit again. I trust in You to help me through this day—not just to survive, but to thrive.

Thank You, Lord Jesus, for Your eternal love and faithfulness to hear my cry and lift me up again. Amen.

PASSING THE TEST

Read: James 1:2–7, 12

Blessed is the man who
perseveres under trial,
because when he has stood the test,
he will receive the crown of life that God
has promised to those who love him.
JAMES 1:12

Why do we give tests in school? The obvious answer is so we can measure our students' mastery of the subject and their skills development. Likewise, James said that life's tests are ways for God to measure the development of our faith and perseverance. Did God leave us to learn these things on our own? No, not at all. In the Gospel of John, Jesus assured the disciples that in His absence the Holy Spirit would come to minister to His believers and teach them the way of truth (see John 14:26).

When I was a student in school, there were numerous occasions when I silently prayed during tests (especially those on algebra and chemistry). Sometimes I prayed believing that God would help me recall important information because I had studied diligently. I believed that He would help me to do my best. Other times I prayed with not so much belief as hope. In those instances when I had not adequately prepared myself, I usually struck out. Notice I said that *I* struck out. God never failed me. I failed. Period.

James points out God's generosity in granting wisdom, provided that we ask for it in faith. If we do not believe God will provide, then His work cannot be completed in us. When we ask in faith, we are submitting to Christ's lordship and allowing Him to be the master. Without that submission, we are putting ourselves in the position of authority, thus hindering the power of God in our lives.

If we ask in faith, we must also live by faith. We need to walk the walk and talk the talk.

Occasionally I have conferred with parents who are so negative that it would be easy to hurl accusations and insults right back at them. Instead, though, I have asked God to prevent the conference from becoming a verbal volleyball match by giving me patience and wisdom. I am always amazed at how God has given me just the right words and attitude to bring about understanding. Try praying before your conferences and see what a difference the Holy Spirit will make.

Heavenly Father, give me strength and wisdom to resist the urge to retaliate when I am under fire. Help me to reach out to those who may be persecuting me and understand their concerns. Bless those who are testing my limits and help me to find ways to reach out to them in sincerity. Amen.

ON BEING PATIENT

Read: Proverbs 14:29; Proverbs 15:18;
Galatians 5:22–23

A patient man has great understanding,
but a quick-tempered man displays folly.
PROVERBS 14:29

Why do people assume that teachers are patient?
So often when I meet someone for the first time,
they comment, "Oh, you're a teacher? You must
be a very patient person!" People assume that I
possess this virtue, as if it is an innate characteristic. To be honest, I find that I am not really a
patient person.

As a Spirit-filled Christian, my life should
exhibit this quality. If I am to be Christlike, I

should be patient. Though He was sometimes tough with those who were not about His Father's business, Jesus was the model of patience with the meek and lowly.

In Proverbs, we see that a patient person is understanding and peaceful. We need this attribute not only when we work with our students but in conferencing with parents, collaborating with our fellow teachers, and even in the teachers' lounge.

Often when parents enter the school with a contentious spirit, they just need someone to listen to them. Being silent when listening to an upset or angry parent speaks volumes. First, it shows that you respect them and their concerns. It also shows that you are in control of yourself and thinking clearly. Letting the parents vent their frustration defuses the tension greatly. By patiently listening, you then can be more empathetic and selective in the words you speak. Being slow to speak also helps you differentiate frustration from hostility. This helps you to forgive the person when it seems that you are being personally attacked. Above all, your patient attitude will be a mirror of God's love.

I have often found that my patience with

children is much greater than with adults who act like children. We understand that children will behave immaturely because they are children. When you are faced with trying circumstances, try breathing a silent prayer for patience and wisdom, and then stop and hear what the other person is saying. After all, *listen* and *silent* are made of the same six letters.

Heavenly Father, forgive me when I am impatient with others. Help me to mirror Your patience and kindness. Help me to remember that often I need someone to be patient with me. Amen.

GRADING PAPERS

Read: Proverbs 12; Acts 7:51

Whoever loves discipline loves knowledge,
but he who hates correction is stupid.
PROVERBS 12:1

As you sit grading Jeff's paper, you wonder how many times it will take for Jeff to get it right. How many reminders will he need to capitalize the first word of each sentence? How many times must he be told to end every sentence with appropriate punctuation? Is he displaying a lack of understanding or just stubbornness?

We all have some faults that need correction. In the Book of Acts, the early Christian leader Stephen, in his speech to the Sanhedrin, called the Jews a "stiff-necked people." If you look up the cross-references for Acts 7:51, you will find that God called the Hebrews stiff-necked on several occasions. Why? They had resisted submission to God and thus lost His blessing.

How many times have I missed God's blessings because I was a stiff-necked fool? (I freely admit to having a stubborn streak a mile wide.) I have failed to witness when I knew God was opening the door for me to share His Word. I could call it shyness, but truthfully, I was unwilling to yield to the Holy Spirit because He was not on the day's agenda. I have clung to bad habits far too many times out of sheer stubbornness, only to miss the blessing of freedom from bondage.

God does not ever force His will on us. He makes it available and invites us to join Him in His work. We often decline the master's invitation only to wallow with the "swine" or have our own pity party. *We* become our own enemies.

We have to remember that just as God does not force us to join Him, but lovingly continues to encourage, so must we lovingly continue to guide our seemingly stiff-necked students to a point of maturity and understanding. Just as God teaches through mistakes, so must we persevere

with the Jeffs of our classroom until they capitalize the start of every sentence.

*Dear Lord, thank You for Your patience
with me. I confess that I am often stubborn
and unwilling to submit to Your authority
and leadership. Forgive me for my stiff-
necked ways and renew my spirit. Lord,
help me remember to mirror Your loving
patience for my students. Amen.*

STANDING ON MY TWO LEFT FEET

Read: 2 Corinthians 4:8–14

We are hard pressed on every side,
but not crushed;
perplexed, but not in despair;
persecuted, but not abandoned;
struck down, but not destroyed.
2 CORINTHIANS 4:8–9

As a child, I fantasized that someday I would be a beautiful ballerina twirling across a stage in toe shoes. Oh, to be a willowy wisp in a tulle tutu! But my genetic code predetermined the outcome of that dream. Instead of inheriting my mother's long lanky legs, I am built like my paternal relatives with a trunk like a redwood and legs like stumps. To add insult to injustice, I am a walking catastrophe!

A few years ago, after I broke my ankle while on a mission trip with the church youth, I was forced to direct Vacation Bible School from a pew with my ankle bandaged and on ice. Even though I was in pain and longed for the comforts of home, I knew there was a job to be done, and our team was depending upon me for leadership. I pressed on (or, in my case, hobbled) to complete the mission. I could not stand on my own, but with God's strength I could go on.

Often we are hindered by our own limitations, and serving God takes a backseat. We are squeezed by the demands of family, friends, graduate school, and career. Additional pressures discourage us from being the servants we are called to be.

Keep both feet firmly planted in the gospel. Continually develop your own Bible study and prayer life. Therein you will find your source of strength for withstanding the daily pressures. Therein will you be enriched and enabled to stand firm and march on victoriously.

Lord, when I am discouraged and ready to abandon the mission You have set before me, give me strength to stand and faith to see it to completion. Amen.

IS IT RECESS YET?

Read: Psalm 40:1–4; Isaiah 40:28–31

I waited patiently for the LORD;
he turned to me and heard my cry.
PSALM 40:1

Some days the time seems to pass before we have scarcely begun our work. Other days pass like a snail on a treadmill, and we long for them to end.

About midterm is usually when I found the days becoming endless. By then the schedules had been settled, the students had gotten into a bit of a routine, and the newness of the term had worn off. Those were the days when little Jimmy would ask every fifteen minutes, "Is it recess yet?" To be truthful, the teachers were wondering the same thing! Yes, teachers need a break, too.

As we find our comfort zones, it is so easy to become complacent—and complacency is the step-sister of boredom and discontent. When we become complacent in our relationship with God, we get our spiritual tires stuck in the mud and muck of daily strife. We need a spiritual recess to refresh us for the daily grind.

However, sometimes we have to wait for God to refresh us. When we turn to God in prayer and cry for help, we must be patient for Him to work in His own time. Why doesn't God answer us instantly? In Psalm 40:3, David says that when God answered his cry and rescued him, He put a new song of praise in David's mouth. The psalmist goes on to say that many will trust the Lord when they see and hear what God has done. God accomplishes His purposes and answers us in His own time so that He may be exalted and glorified.

Be patient in those seemingly endless days when you are feeling weary and in need of a break. Know that God will enable you to stand, to walk, to run, and to soar in order to bring glory to Him.

*Lord, may Your name be exalted when I am
exhausted. Lift me up and give me renewed
strength of mind, body, and soul. May all
the credit and praise and glory be Yours.
Amen.*

PSALM 23

(Paraphrased for the Teacher)

The Lord is my superglue; I shall not fall apart.
He makes me go out in the hall to count to ten;
    He leads me to the teachers' lounge for
        refuge.
He guides me in single-file lines to the cafeteria
    and keeps order.
Even though I walk through the valley of
    bus duty,
    I will fear no evil,
    for He is with me;
His rod and staff comfort and protect me.

He prepares a conference table before me in the
 presence of anxious parents.
He anoints my head with wisdom and fills my
 mouth with gracious words.
Surely goodness and mercy will follow me all
 the days of my life,
And I will someday dwell in retirement knowing
 I have served the Lord, and He held me
 together!

Dedicated to the teachers
at Brewbaker Primary School, 1981–1998

PART V

INVEST IN OTHERS

A PRAYER FOR THE WORKPLACE

Precious and holy heavenly Father, I thank You for a new day. I praise You for Your creation and for Your unfailing mercies to me.

Heavenly Father, I am thankful for this career to which You have called me. I thank You for the economic security this job brings to my family.

Lord, thank You for my coworkers. So many have been encouragers to me in times of frustration, distress, and grief. I see You shining through the lives of many of these people each day, bringing joy to the students and staff. Bless these committed Christians and equip them as they serve You daily.

Father, I also thank You for opportunities to minister to those around me each day. Help me to be an encourager to those who feel hopeless. Give me an understanding of my coworkers' needs and help me see how I can minister to them. Lord, if there is one particular person to whom I should especially be kind, lay it on my heart so that I may know Your will.

Forgive me, Lord, when I fail to speak or act as You would have me to do. Forgive my apathy when I am so consumed with my own business. Forgive my quick tongue and unthinking mind when I spout off at people. Forgive me for not valuing each person as much as You do.

Help me to be a better witness for You this day, Lord. Amen.

THE GIFT OF ENCOURAGEMENT

Read: Hebrews 3:12–15

But encourage one another daily,
as long as it is called Today,
so that none of you may be hardened
by sin's deceitfulness.
HEBREWS 3:13

It had been an exhausting morning. By ten o'clock I had been called away from my students to help with crises in the office three times, taken two calls from very anxious parents, and received a memo that an important report to the special education director was overdue. Then came the call from my mother to let me know that Daddy needed to be hospitalized. My nerves were raw, tears were welling in my eyes, and I felt I would fall apart at any moment.

In haste I scribbled a note to one of my Christian coworkers and prayer warriors, Kris, asking her to breathe a prayer for me. Within minutes a child appeared with a note in hand that today is tucked in my Bible. Kris wrote back, " 'Praise be the LORD, for he has heard my cry for mercy. The LORD is my strength and my shield; my heart trusts in him, and I am helped.' Psalm 28:6–7. HANG IN THERE!" That note of encouragement in God's Word gave me the strength to handle the rest of the day.

Again, today, I sit amazed at the timeliness of encouraging messages. I have been blessed with many Christian colleagues and friends who seem inspired to send words of comfort, strength, and encouragement when I need them most. The most recent example occurred when this manuscript was due in a few weeks, and I was frustrated by a case of writer's block. One anxious morning, I found myself sobbing during my prayer time. Gradually, though, the anxiety began to wash away into the tears, and a calmness came over me like a gentle wave breaking over my feet. At that moment, for no particular reason, I went to the computer and checked my E-mail.

There was a message from my friend and colleague of many years, Althea. The subject line drew me in like a bee to nectar. It said: "WHATCHA WORRYING 'BOUT?" Althea began by writing, "God has it under control!" Then she cited passages from Matthew, Philippians, and Psalms, reminding me of my temporary lack of faith in the One who called me to write this book. The conclusion was this passage from Isaiah 41:10: "So do not fear, for I am with you; do not be dismayed, for I am your God. . . . I will uphold you with my righteous right hand."

Wow! What an answer to prayer!

Teaching can be a lonely profession. Sometimes we are isolated from other adults except for a few minutes in the cafeteria or lounge. I urge you to take time to encourage one another. When you know someone is struggling, be ready to offer a kind word or write a note to let her know of your concern. Share a Scripture and offer to pray for her or him.

Lord, thank You for creating humans with

the capacity and need for fellowship. You are more gracious to me than I deserve. Thank You for special friends who share Your Holy Word and bless them as they reach out to others. Help me to be more sensitive to opportunities to encourage. Amen.

IN NEED OF COMFORTING

Read: 2 Corinthians 1:3–7

Praise be to the God and Father
of our Lord Jesus Christ,
the Father of compassion
and the God of all comfort,
who comforts us in all our troubles,
so that we can comfort those
in any trouble with the comfort
we ourselves have received from God.
2 CORINTHIANS 1:3–4

Have you ever had one of those weeks that made
you want to curl up in a corner and cry? Once, in
the span of four days, four teachers at my school
had deaths in their families. Most of us had

worked together for fifteen to twenty years. The bond that is forged over the years made our empathy deeper and more personal. Even the newest faculty members turned out to attend the funerals and reach out to the hurting families.

In the midst of this very emotional week, two students had grandparents die. Each of these little boys sat and sobbed on my shoulder. Their parents were finding it difficult to explain death to these eight year olds, but the hurting children needed to know something.

The boys were disturbed about their grandmothers being "covered with dirt." As I walked on the playground with one boy, struggling with my own emotions and trying to reassure him, a butterfly fluttered by us. That gave me an idea. I explained that we have two parts to us—our bodies, or earth suits, and our souls. Like a caterpillar that has spun a warm cocoon around itself and then one day breaks out as a winged creature, freer and more capable than before, so had his grandmother left her earth suit and flown to heaven. The beautiful part of her that he loved so dearly was her soul, and that part of her was alive in heaven with Jesus.

As educators, we have choices to make each

day. While court decrees have made us hesitant to share our Christian faith with students, we still can honor God when we seize everyday opportunities to share His love and truths. When we reach out and share the burdens of others, we all draw a little nearer to God.

Lord, help me to seize the opportunities to minister to others. Help me to remember that when I have done it unto the least of these, I have done it unto Thee. Amen.

A WORTHWHILE INVESTMENT

Read: Proverbs 20:12; James 1:19

My dear brothers, take note of this:
Everyone should be quick to listen,
slow to speak and slow to become angry.
JAMES 1:19

Frequently I would tell my more talkative students that because they have two ears and one mouth, they should therefore listen twice as much as they talk. While this platitude is easy to dispense, sometimes it's had to practice. Yet, as Christians in the schools, we have a unique opportunity to minister through the fine art of listening.

Our students need a safe person with whom to share their thoughts, fears, hopes, and dreams.

Sometimes those thoughts shared in passing between classes are one student's way of testing us to
see if we are paying attention. She may initially say
something shocking to see if you are listening. A
nonjudgmental and warm response may give her
the signal to approach you in confidence. Sometimes students are in crisis. Sometimes they just
need a positive role model and someone to trust.
Your listening ear is a great gift.

Many times colleagues dropped by my room
after school. Often they interrupted some planning or paperwork I was trying to complete, apol-
ogizing for the interruption. Yet in their lingering,
I sensed a need. I would rather stop what I was
doing and listen to my friends than ignore them.
Sometimes they needed to vent the inherent frustrations that had accumulated during the school
day. Some days they needed to divulge a confidence and cry on my shoulder. Other times there
was a success story or a joke to share.

In a world of hurry and wait, voice mail, faxes,
and E-mail, we all still crave human contact. Each
of us needs to feel there is a safe haven where we
are valued and understood. On my file cabinet
was a magnet that proclaimed, "Teaching is a
work of the heart." So is listening.

Dear Lord, I am so thankful that You hear my prayers, voiced and unspoken. Help me to be a patient and compassionate listener for those in need of a caring heart. Thank You for those friends who have been available when I needed a listening ear. Amen.

BERRIES, BRIARS,
AND FORGIVENESS

Read: Colossians 3:12–17

Bear with each other and
forgive whatever grievances
you may have against one another.
Forgive as the Lord forgave you.
COLOSSIANS 3:13

It's easy to pick berries if there's no briar patch. While berries are the same whether harvested from the briar patch or along a hedgerow, we appreciate the fruits yielded from the briar patch a little more because we know how hard they were to pick.

Likewise, it's easy to be compassionate, kind,

humble, gentle, and patient as long as life is going smoothly and we are treated well by others. But these traits are much more difficult to display when we have been offended. As hard as we may try, we cannot let these traits shine in us if we hold a grudge against someone. To bear with one another and to forgive someone is hard, especially when we see the offending person on a daily basis.

Human nature wants to be in control and find ways to get even. However, holding a grudge will drain our energy, keeping us on a treadmill of resentment.

To forgive as Christ forgave us is to love the offender in spite of what he or she has done. To truly forgive as Christ forgives is to forget, or at least put it aside so that it does not consume us. That is probably the hardest part of forgiving. Only when we forgive are we able to move forward toward restoring the relationship and allowing the wounds to heal. Had Christ not died and forgiven us, our relationship with our heavenly Father could never be restored.

An unforgiving spirit is much like a briar embedded under the skin, which left unattended will fester and cause pain. Do you have any briars to pluck from your heart today?

Father, help me to forgive those who have hurt me. I know that until I forgive them, You cannot forgive me. Lead me to find a way to reach out to my offender and begin the restoration of our relationship. Thank You for Your gift of forgiveness. Amen.

THE TIME-OUT CORNER

Read: Hebrews 12:4–11

Because the Lord disciplines those he loves,
and he punishes everyone he accepts as a son.
HEBREWS 12:6

Several years ago, my brother and his wife served as
foster parents for an adorable pair of siblings. In all
honesty, they were the most beautiful and most
hyperactive children I have ever seen! When he
was in kindergarten, little Johnny usually went to
the time-out chair at least once each day. Unstruc-
tured times, however, were even more challenging
to him. At a family dinner at Grandmother and
Papa's house, Johnny repeatedly disobeyed my
brother and was sent to stand in a corner for five

minutes. During his fourth visit to the corner, Johnny turned to the family and emphatically announced, "You know, it's not very much fun standing in this corner!"

If we are honest with ourselves, we have all had some unpleasant visits to the time-out corner. As an adult, I must admit that God takes me aside to His time-out corner occasionally. Yes, God is the great disciplinarian, but I do not see Him as vengeful or unloving. When my parents had to discipline me as a child, I never questioned their love for me. I knew they had my best interests at heart. Even more than my parents, God loves me and knows what is best for me.

Look at God as a disciplinary role model. Starting with Adam and Eve, God set boundaries and limitations for their benefit. When they disobeyed and ate the forbidden fruit, punishment was immediate. While God the Father voiced His displeasure, He was still loving. Later, when God punished the children of Israel time and time again, the punishments fit their misdeeds. God is the Father of second chances. He even sacrificed His only Son, Jesus Christ, to give humankind a second chance, an opportunity for salvation that was first extended to Israel.

Discipline and love are complementary. Can you put into practice some of these principles of discipline in your classroom or home today? Set the boundaries, make the consequences immediate, and be ready to give a second chance.

⌁

Heavenly Father, thank You for Your immeasurable love. Thank You for disciplining me when I need it. I praise You because You are the one true God, the God of second chances. Thank You for not giving up on me when I mess up. Amen.

BLESS THE CHILDREN

God bless the children,
Bless them one and all—
Ones in wheelchairs
And ones standing tall.
God bless the ones who really yearn
To do their best but slowly learn,
The one who aces the history quiz
And the one who's not a natural whiz.
Help each child to understand
Genius is not the measure of a man.
Help them know their worth is true
Because they're made in the image of You.
Help me show them that success
Is not measured in more or less
But in the choices that they live
And how much of themselves they give.

SOWING SEEDS OF KINDNESS

Read: 2 Corinthians 9:6–15

And God is able to make
all grace abound to you,
so that in all things at all times,
having all that you need,
you will abound in every good work.
2 CORINTHIANS 9:8

God has placed you in your present workplace for a specific reason. Sometimes the reason is readily recognized, while at other times the answer is not so obvious. Look around you and consider how your spiritual gifts and unique talents can be used to sow seeds of grace. The possibilities are almost endless, as are the rewards.

Perhaps God needs you to be an encourager to a coworker who is struggling with professional issues or personal burdens.

Addressing more practical concerns, God may lay it upon your heart to quietly offer clothing and household items to a student's family whose parents have been laid off work. Perhaps God will lead you to share monetarily with a family whose home has been destroyed.

God may want you in this particular place because He knows the parents of certain students will need your special love and encouragement. You may be able to counsel a child's parents, giving them wisdom for parenting and inviting them to church. Maybe you could serve as a mentor to a young parent who is struggling to complete her education and get a job.

My greatest reward in teaching came about because of Mattie, who has allowed me to share her story. When I first met Mattie, her tears of concern and frustration over her oldest son's school problems touched my heart. She was a single parent, divorced, and living in a rough housing project, dependent upon welfare programs. Substance abuse, as well as physical abuse, had been part of her past. As she wept, she asked me, "What is the answer? Where do I turn?" I took her hand in mine and said, "I don't know all the answers, but I do know the One who does. I will pray for you and your children."

A year later this precious lady came into my room with a radiant smile and tears of gratitude. "I have to thank you for helping me get my life on track," she said. "When I first met you, you said you'd pray for me. After I got home that day, I thought about that. Nobody ever told me that before. I thought I might as well try God. I had tried everything else. A friend started coming by to get us for church since I didn't have a car. Now my children and I all know the Lord. I have my first steady job and a car. I am saving money to make a down payment on a house. Thank you for praying for us."

There is no joy to match this. I have kept in touch with this family over the years. Her oldest son, who struggled so hard in first grade, is now an honors student and playing football. Mattie absolutely glows with the light of the Lord, and God has brought a fine Christian man into her life. Her family was transformed not by me but by the work of the Holy Spirit as I interceded for them. I was merely available to minister to her as the Lord led me.

God, give me sensitivity to the needs around me each day. Fill me with compassion and courage as I risk getting involved in others' lives. Thank You for the joy of serving others. Help me to serve with a spirit of humility. Amen.

HEALING WOUNDS

Read: 2 Peter 1:7; Colossians 3:12–14;
Ephesians 4:31–32

Get rid of all bitterness, rage and anger,
brawling and slander,
along with every form of malice.
Be kind and compassionate to one another,
forgiving each other,
just as in Christ God forgave you.
EPHESIANS 4:31–32

It's May, and at school everyone is anxious for summer vacation. The children, who are in the throes of spring fever, are reaching a saturation point, and the beautiful spring weather beckons them outdoors like a siren's song to sailors.

Needless to say, teachers are ready for that summer break, too. (After all, the three best reasons for teaching are June, July, and August!) Nerves are on edge and patience with one another is sometimes short. We allow minor irritations to become festering sores in our spirits. We nurse grudges until they become full-grown monsters.

Yes, we are every bit as human as the children we teach. However, as the adults in charge, we have a tremendous responsibility to be positive role models for the students. Children are extremely perceptive, and they know when there is friction between adults. How we choose to resolve our differences will impact them. If we gossip, backstab, bicker, and criticize, how can we expect our students to handle differences constructively?

Let's remember that many eyes and ears are observing us. Make peace with one another. Forgive past hurts and bury grudges, even if the other person is unwilling to make amends. I am only responsible for my own actions and attitudes. If I have apologized and tried to make peace, then I have done my part. This is especially important as the school term ends. Don't let ill will grow and fester over the summer break. Try to sweep out the dust bunnies of anger, jealousy, gossip, prejudice, and misunderstanding before you leave the campus for your well-deserved vacation.

Father God, I confess that I have been impatient and treated others wrongly. Forgive me, God, for allowing myself to be consumed with selfishness, pride, and prejudice. Help those whom I have wronged to also forgive me. Help me to forgive those who have mistreated me. Amen.

PART VI

REFLECT

BLOOM WHERE YOU ARE PLANTED

Read: Philippians 4:10–13

I can do everything through him
who gives me strength.
PHILIPPIANS 4:13

As I look out the window, I can't deny that my usually full flower bed looks rather anemic. I can water and fertilize, weed and spray, but the searing heat of this summer has taken its toll.

Teaching is much like gardening. We must nourish and protect each student. We are expected to find the right nutrients (phonics, whole language, math exploration, and so on) to help students grow and develop academically. We are asked to teach positive values and good social skills to encourage their emotional growth. The expectations that teachers face can be overwhelming.

While we are tending to our students' needs, we may suffer from neglect if we are not careful. Teaching requires a large investment of oneself; it is physically, emotionally, mentally, and spiritually draining at times. And while some of you may be blessed with a strong support system, realistically, family members and friends may be very loving, but they too are busy and exhausted. If you are like me, you may experience burnout phases. Some of you may be experiencing a mid-life crisis, questioning your choice of career.

We can easily let negativism taint our perspective. Here, then, is a plan to reverse that downward spiral. First, sort out the reasons for your dissatisfaction. Decide which situations are within your control and work to change those things. For those unchangeable factors, seek advice and tangible help from others—and then release them to God and leave them in His hands. You can and should seek His wisdom and intervention to change things. The weeds of negativism will choke your garden's prize blooms. Only by weeding out the negative ideas can those blooms (creativity, enthusiasm, cooperation, professionalism) flourish.

To fertilize your spirit, you need to do some things for yourself. Set a time just for yourself each day, even if it is only fifteen minutes. If it means getting up a little earlier, do it. Exercise, have an ongoing hobby, take a square dance class, read a book, or just take a long, hot bubble bath. Find something you will enjoy. Above all, stay grounded in God's Word. If you are not already involved in a Bible study, I encourage you to do so. Sharing your beliefs and burdens with fellow Christians will help you maintain a more balanced perspective. Then you will be able to bloom where you are planted.

Lord, give me a spirit of true contentment that does not depend on my circumstances. Give me insight and wisdom as I learn and grow in Your grace. Amen.

DIAL 1-800-DESIRES

Read: Psalm 37:3–6

Delight yourself in the LORD
and he will give you
the desires of your heart.
PSALM 37:4

There's an old Rolling Stones hit song from the 1960s that laments, "I can't get no satisfaction." That statement still sums up the attitude of so many even in this new century. Life is about getting what I want, whatever the cost. (I can almost hear you say, "If I wanted to be rich, I would not be teaching.") Even teachers become easily caught on the treadmill of wishing, wanting, and working to acquire things.

God does not condemn new homes, auto-mobiles, boats, designer clothes, and other material trappings, nor does He promise us these things. But the psalmist said that God will give us the desires of our hearts. Is this a contradiction?

The first five words of this verse state a condition upon which the promise hinges. What does it mean to delight oneself in the Lord? Delight implies happiness, pleasure, and joy. *Roget's Thesaurus* lists *satisfy* and *content* as synonyms for the verb *delight*. To delight in the Lord involves a purposeful choice of will and attitude. Whenever my heart's desires are in line with His, there is peace, joy, and contentment. There is a level of satisfaction that is unequalled.

To reach that state of contentment requires surrender of self. Through prayer, my will must be dissolved and reshaped. No longer can I use prayer as a spiritual remote control, trying to commandeer God. God will do what God will do! Who am I to think that by praying for selfish reasons I can gain God's favor? Whenever I have aligned my heart's desires with God's heart, I know His promise is true. He will give me the pure desires of my heart that are in His will. God does not promise us perfect health, worldly wealth, or fame. He does promise to supply our needs just as He does for the birds of the air, and He does promise His eternal love and presence. In the end, what more can I desire?

Lord, forgive me for my stubborn and selfish will. Help me to draw near to You and align my heart with Yours. Help me to rest and rejoice in the promise that You will bless me with the desires of my heart. Amen.

BURNOUT 911

Read: 2 Corinthians 4:16–18

Therefore we do not lose heart.
Though outwardly we are wasting away,
yet inwardly we are being
renewed day by day.
2 CORINTHIANS 4:16

I can't take it anymore! I want out of here right now! I'm losing my mind! Calgon, take me away! Is anyone listening? I have to have a change now!

Perhaps you, too, are at the end of your rope. A counselor friend told me that most teachers experience a burnout phase every seven to ten years. How do you keep going?

The apostle Paul's words offer some solid

advice to the frustrated and frazzled. First, do not lose heart. In other words, don't give up. Don't surrender and wave the white flag. Don't lose your courage or will to go on. You may feel that you are losing the battle, but the war is not over! Mount your steed and charge back into the fray! In the physical sense, your heart is what sustains life. Spiritually and emotionally, your heart is the spirit of life that you bring into all you do.

Paul's imagery of outwardly wasting away while inwardly being renewed each day reminds me of a snake shedding its skin. As the snake writhes and wriggles trying to work its way out of the old skin, it appears to be tormented. Yet, underneath it has a lovely new snakeskin belt to show off. On our deepest, darkest days we may look rather pathetic, but let's keep focused on Christ so we can be inwardly renewed through prayer, Bible study, and fellowship with other believers.

Our earthly frustrations and problems are temporary. In the grand scheme of things, this is just a blip on God's big screen. We can't see the end results or the rewards that await us. However, we are to gaze through eyes of hope toward our eternal reward.

So, you're ready to throw in the towel? You

don't think you can hang on any longer? Tie a knot in the end of your rope, hang on, and don't lose heart. There is hope for better times.

Lord, I am so grateful You didn't give me a crystal ball. I know in Your infinite wisdom You knew that I could not handle seeing the whole picture all at once. You are my hope and strength and joy. Hold me together today and give me the strength and will to hang on awhile longer. Amen.

A PRAYER OF
ENCOURAGEMENT

My friend, I prayed for you today.
I thanked God for you and what you mean to me.

I asked the Lord to bless you:
    to give you good health,
    to grant you peace, and
    to give you the desires of your heart.

I asked God to help you:
to strengthen you in your faith,
to guide your steps,
to keep you from harm,
to help you know His will for you.

I thanked the Lord:
for the many times you have encouraged me,
for the many prayers you have lifted in my behalf,
for the joy of your friendship and fellowship
in this workplace.

HOW TO TAKE CHRIST
OUT OF CHRISTMAS

Read: John 10:7–15

*The thief comes only to
steal and kill and destroy;
I have come that they may have life,
and have it to the full.*
JOHN 10:10

As I sit alone in the soft glow of the tree lights,
my mind is racing. Did I remember my close
friends? Have I mailed Christmas letters to everyone on the list? Have I wrapped everything?
Who was it that I planned to give baked goods?
When is that party? What shall I wear? When is
the Christmas concert? Did I invite the family?

The beautifully wrapped packages, the garlands and bows so carefully hung, and the tree decorations glistening and twinkling have lost their appeal. In a matter of minutes, they have been reduced to chores on a seemingly endless list. I find myself secretly wishing the holiday would be over soon. Exhaustion has replaced the exhilaration I once enjoyed. How is it that I have lost the joy of this beautiful season?

For one thing, my life was a shopping nightmare. I had to get all of the shopping done before we got out of school for the holidays, and besides, I wanted to take advantage of those great sales. I knew if I waited past the twentieth of December the crowds would be terrible, and I had to find just the right gifts for everyone, even a few people I am not especially fond of. They usually get me something, and I have to keep the score even.

Then almost every day of the calendar was filled. I really had to attend Marge's party since I had the flu and missed it last year. I had to go to the school PTA Christmas program and show support for my students. I had to attend the church's Christmas cantata—after all, I *am* in the choir. I had to go to the faculty party since I signed up to be a secret pal. I had to go with Joe

175

to his store's Christmas party. Of course, I had to attend Ben's recital. What kind of mom would miss that? I had to share the spirit of the season with the needy and give some time at the Salvation Army. I had to bake cookies for some of my closest friends. And then I promised I would help wrap and deliver gifts with the youth, too.

Were any of these activities wrong? As I gaze upon the ceramic holy family displayed on the table, I realize that for all my good intentions, all I really have to do to celebrate Christmas is worship the Lord. I have left Christ out of Christmas, replacing worship with overcommitment and sacrifice with commercialism. Is this the abundant life to which my Lord has called me?

Dear Lord, please forgive me for becoming so busy doing things that I forgot what You came to earth to accomplish. I lost focus of You and Your purpose, as well as my purpose. Restore to me the sense that I have been created to fellowship with You and worship and bring glory to You. Restore to me the joy of my salvation. Thank You, Lord. Amen.

IN THE SIGH OF THE LORD

Read: James 4:7–10

Humble yourselves before the Lord,
and he will lift you up.
JAMES 4:10

Recently I saw this blooper on a church marquee: "Humble yourself in the sigh of the Lord." What a difference a T makes! While I couldn't help but chuckle, I wondered aloud, "How many times have I come before the Lord, broken and in a mess, and made God sigh?" Thankfully, God still loves me and puts my life together again. I can just hear our patient Lord saying, "Haven't I told you not to be so stubborn?"

The truth in this verse is that unless we do

humble ourselves before the Lord, we are incomplete. When we are broken in spirit or when our bodies are tormented in pain, God can restore us and lift us to higher ground. In 2 Chronicles 7:14, the writer says that God will hear our prayers, forgive us, and bring healing when we humble ourselves before Him.

All of those benefits are appealing to me, but just how exactly do I humble myself before God? Scripture says we must pray, seek God's face, and repent of our sins. Okay, I can pray, but a deeper examination of the Scriptures will show that I must pray in the right spirit, trusting Him as a little child. If I seek God's face, I will do what is pleasing to Him and what honors Him. I will seek to know His will. The third key to being humble is repentance, or making an about-face from the old ways, thoughts, and attitudes to reflect a pure heart.

I recognize that none of this is possible without God's help. I must petition God and ask in childlike faith for His help. I must surrender my will to His. Then I can humble myself in God's sight—and maybe He won't sigh too deeply this time!

Lord, thank You for loving me even when I must surely exasperate and disappoint You with my sins. Please forgive me and restore me. Amen.

BARE STRENGTH

Read: 2 Corinthians 12:7–10

*"My grace is sufficient for you,
for my power is made perfect in weakness."*
2 CORINTHIANS 12:9

Sunset is an amazing time of day to me. (Sunrise is not on my daily agenda.) I love to watch God's canvas as He paints vibrant shades of blue, coral, and violet that then melt into luscious opalescent hues of pink, lavender, and melon. In every sunset I see a different design, an ever-changing horizon influenced by the season's landscapes.

In the bleakness of winter, for example, I am captivated by the mural of silhouetted bare trees against a coral and violet horizon. When I was young, I disliked winter because the trees were bare. Now I appreciate the temporary absence of the foliage, for in looking at the bare trees, I see a truth about nature and about God.

In 1995, Hurricane Opal surprised central and northern Alabama with winds of eighty-five to one hundred miles per hour throughout a very long and harrowing night. I remember vividly the shock when morning came and daylight washed over the devastated landscape. A beautiful pecan grove in the lot behind us had been leveled overnight. All of those beautiful grand trees were uprooted and toppled like dominoes. Even the huge oaks on our property were uprooted and laid across our yard like matchsticks. At the same time, many of the tall spindly trees had withstood the howling winds. I learned that the tall lofty branches of the oaks and pecans had been caught up much like an umbrella in a gust of wind. Their dense foliage had also worked to their disadvantage when the leafy boughs were drenched. The spindly trees had withstood the winds because they had so little to weigh them down; they could bend without breaking.

God's power in our lives is most evident in our times of weakness and vulnerability. Just as the toppled trees were weighed down by their beautiful foliage, so are we encumbered by our delusions of self-sufficiency. Sometimes a limb breaks because it has become too heavy. Are we not the same? We try to juggle too many things, and the strain causes us to crack under pressure. Sometimes we try to do so much in our strength that even a small gust may cause an upheaval.

Just as the trees of winter can withstand the winds because they are stripped bare, so can we withstand the gales of life when we strip ourselves of our pride, vanity, and stubbornness. For in our vulnerability, God's glory, power, and strength are revealed like the radiant sunset through the silhouettes of winter's bare trees.

Oh, God! Forgive me of my pride. Forgive me for trying to do everything in my own strength and not relying on You. How foolish I am for thinking I can make it on my own. Lord, I lay myself at Your feet and ask that in my weakness now Your strength may be made perfect. Amen.

PROBLEMS? HERE'S HOPE!

Read: Isaiah 40:8; Mark 13:31; John 3:16

Heaven and earth will pass away,
but my words will never pass away.
MARK 13:31

Some of my friends have nicknamed me Job, and since then I have considered forming a Job Fan Club or support group. When troubles seem to pile up at my door, I know that my problems are not nearly as severe as those Job endured.

Still, it often feels like the world is crashing in around me. My dad's health has been so poor for many years that we felt sure they would name a wing of the new hospital in his honor. (Somehow the hospital has not yet done this.) We have had so many family members on the church prayer list that the secretary actually called one time because we did not have anyone listed. One of my dear friends says that she keeps a whole page in her prayer journal just for my family's needs, and she keeps it dog-eared for easy reference!

But trouble is no laughing matter when you are dealing with it. Sometimes you wonder if the heartache will ever end. Will the massive dark cloud hanging over your head ever disappear?

God's good news is that the only thing everlasting is His Word. His Word is truth, light, and love to you and me. His promise is to love us eternally. That love brings peace to us in our times of trial. As a friend once reminded me (when I was lamenting our ongoing family crises), when it says in God's Word "it came to pass," it refers to times of plagues, trials, and diverse hardships. However, he reminded me that God's love and Word came to stay. We can bank on that!

Isn't it a joy to know that our problems and sorrows will not stay forever, but that God's love will endure the ages? As you struggle with your burdens, look to the Lord Jesus and anticipate better days with the confidence that He will be with you always.

Dear God, I praise You for being the One constant force in this universe. Thank You for always being with me, even when I feel alone. Thank You for lifting my burdens when I cry out to You. Thank You for Your strength that carries me through each crisis. You know the needs of my family, and I ask You to meet those needs. Amen.

PART VII

EXPERIENCE GOD

TO BE A TREE

Read: Psalm 1:3; Psalm 92:12–15;
Jeremiah 17:7–8

But blessed is the man who
trusts in the LORD,
whose confidence is in him.
He will be like a tree planted by the water
that sends out its roots by the stream.
It does not fear when heat comes;
its leaves are always green.
It has no worries in a year of drought,
and never fails to bear fruit.
JEREMIAH 17:7–8

Lord, I want to be an evergreen
Tall and majestic and leafy,

Giving shade and rest
To the weary.

Lord, I want to be a fruit tree,
Full and fragrant
With the sweetness of Your
Spirit's fruit in my life.

Lord, I want to be a palm tree
Swaying gracefully in the breeze,
Bowing humbly in the storm
But rising again in the new morn.

Lord, I want to be a redwood
Grand and immovable,
Standing strong through years
Reaching heavenward to glorify You.

Lord, I want to be a cypress,
Rooted deeply by the stream,
Constantly being nourished by
Your living waters.

"ACCEPT NO SUBSTITUTES"

Read: Joshua 24:13–16

But if serving the LORD
seems undesirable to you,
then choose for yourselves
this day whom you will serve. . . .
But as for me and my household,
we will serve the LORD.
JOSHUA 24:15

One of the hallmark characteristics of my learning disabled students was their strong desire and
need for familiarity and sameness of routine. They
were, indeed, creatures of habit. They especially
protested loudly when I was absent. One student
explained why he did not cooperate with the

191

substitute teacher: "I just don't know if I can trust her. I don't know if she is for real."

As I considered this child's perspective, I asked myself how many times have I misplaced my trust in persons or things that were not "for real." I have put my trust in my own abilities far too many times. As a beginning teacher, I put my trust in my own strength and abilities. I was energetic, creative, and enthusiastic. Sleep, personal interests, and family took a backseat when I had a sudden burst of creativity. I would spend countless hours making bulletin boards and games. Working on my own strength eventually led to a severe burnout phase. I could no longer function on my strength.

As educators, we have so many demands made upon our time and resources. Certainly I would not advocate neglecting professional duties. God has called you to this honorable profession. However, it is imperative to prioritize how we invest our energy and time. We have personal needs that must be met. We have families and friends who need our time and attention. We cannot forget our service to God through our churches, either. We are pulled in so many directions, creating confusion, frustration, and guilt.

What does God require? God's priority list is

found in Exodus 20. It is no coincidence that the first commandment God decreed concerned keeping Him first: "You shall have no other gods before me" (Exodus 20:3). God expects to be first in our lives. Anything that is given a higher priority than worshiping God—jobs, hobbies, sports, and even family—is against His will. God created humans to fellowship with Him and worship Him.

Jesus' Sermon on the Mount (Matthew 6:33) spells out what the Christian's first priority ought to be: seeking God's kingdom and righteousness. When we do this, Jesus promised, everything else will fall into place. As I continually renew my commitment to God and seek His will, my priorities become much clearer. I may have a house that would make Martha Stewart scream—there may be weeds in my flower beds or dishes left overnight in the sink!—but when I prioritize and serve God, life is simplified. I am blessed with His peace and joy and strength for daily living. Choose this day whom you will serve.

Holy Father, help me to seek Your kingdom first and to accept no substitutes. Forgive me for allowing other areas of my life to crowd You out. Amen.

WORSHIP OR "WORKSHIP"?

Read: Exodus 20:3; Ephesians 2:8–10;
Romans 12:1–2

Therefore, I urge you, brothers,
in view of God's mercy,
to offer your bodies as living sacrifices,
holy and pleasing to God—
this is your spiritual act of worship.
ROMANS 12:1

What is your passion in life? Admiration? Wealth?
Fame? A certain kind of car? A bigger home? To
have the most intelligent and talented kids? To be
on the most committees? To be Super Parent and
Super Spouse?

At different stages in my life, I have allowed

other people and things to become my passion, relegating God to a little corner in my cluttered heart. As a young woman in college, my passion was the pursuit of a young man I dated. I wanted to be married more than anything in the world! As a beginning teacher, my focus shifted to my work, and school became my life.

Because I am a people pleaser by nature, I have allowed my desire to please and appease to overshadow my spiritual growth and worship. I was faithful to the church but not to God. I was working on umpteen committees but not truly worshiping God.

Don't misunderstand what I am saying. Many of the things that we spend our time and energy doing and pursuing are good, and some may even be noble causes. Certainly the Lord desires that we use our abilities to serve Him and others. However, there is a fine line that defines what we worship in our hearts. When we become so busy or consumed with something that it crowds out God, then our activity has become our idol.

The challenge for us as Christians is to keep a healthy balance between our works and worship. True worship of our heavenly Father will prompt us to work. The works are a natural by-product of our strong relationship with God. Make time daily to study God's Word and meditate. Talk to God frequently and ask Him to bless you in your works. Worship the Lord with your life. It isn't just a Sunday activity.

Lord, help me to keep a healthy balance in my life and to always keep You first. You have promised that if we seek You first and Your righteousness, You will bless us. I trust Your promise. Help me to worship You with all of my life, and help me to not let my work come before You. Amen.

NAME YOUR MASTER

Read: John 8:31–41

Jesus said, "If you hold to my teaching,
you are really my disciples.
Then you will know the truth,
and the truth will set you free."
JOHN 8:31–32

As the class discussed the Civil War, attention
was turned to the reasons why slavery was wrong.
Someone pointed out that although the slaves
were owned by landowners, they had no privileges
as family members and no legal or civil rights. They
were just property. Yet despite the slaves' limited
opportunities for improving their circumstances
through education, they were able to compose some

of the most moving music of the era—the great Negro spirituals. Clearly, their souls were not in bondage.

What enslaves you? Are you bound by guilt? Do the unconfessed sins of your past hold you back and rob you of the joy in life? Confess those sins that you have buried and allow yourself to be set free.

Are you chained to your present station in life by your fear of change? Recognize your God-given talents, and seek to utilize them in new and creative ways that will honor God. Claim God's promises and step out in bold faith to accomplish all that He has for you.

Have you been trapped in a lair of your own making? Is there some unhealthy habit or attitude you have developed and clung to? Perhaps it is alcohol or drugs. Maybe you are enslaved by gluttony or lust. Whether your problem is physical or psychological, if it prevents you from being all that God intends for you to be, it is sin and needs to be eradicated.

Many of us, including myself, recognize our shackles. (My personal slave master is food. Eating is not a sin, but eating the wrong kinds of foods and in large portions is sin.) Yet, there are some whose pride will blind them from recognizing their own forms of bondage. Many people attend church and give generously. They may serve faithfully in various ministries of the church. These are wonderful activities and gestures of goodwill, but they may be done without love. Perhaps some people have unconfessed pride that is preventing them from being free to receive the joyful inheritance and freedom in acknowledging Jesus Christ as Lord.

I challenge you to examine yourself and name your master. If your master is not Jesus Christ, confess this and seek His face. Then you will be set free.

Jesus, I want You to be the One and only master of me. I recommit myself to Your lordship in all areas of my life and ask for Your strength to conquer the bad habits that have controlled me. Thank You for Your forgiveness and love. Amen.

JUMP-START THE DAY

Read: Acts 1:4–8; Romans 12:1–2

He said to them ". . .But you will receive
power when the Holy Spirit comes on you;
and you will be my witnesses in Jerusalem,
and in all Judea and Samaria,
and to the ends of the earth."
ACTS 1:7–8

Are you a morning person? Do you awaken and say, "Good morning, Lord," or do you open one eye and groan, "Oh, no, it's morning"? My family understands that conversation with me occurs only after I have a cup of coffee. I need that caffeine to jump-start my brain cells, open my eyes, and formulate intelligible speech.

Spiritually, I also need a jump-start each day. I confess that at times I allow the worries of the day, poor time management, and last-minute parental duties to distract me. I rush to work like a quarterback without a game plan. I know that the rest of the day will likely go willy-nilly because I have omitted a key component of my preparation.

You see, if I don't first focus on Jesus Christ and ask the Lord to help me renew my mind and prioritize the day according to His will, I am adrift. I have to make a conscious choice to invest that time in prayer and Bible study and chart my course or choose to drift slightly off course like a sailboat with no wind. When I start my day with the Lord, my sails are full and the course is charted for me.

In studying the New Testament, especially the Book of Acts, it is apparent that the Holy Spirit energized those early Christians. Indeed, the Holy Spirit motivated and encouraged them to complete the mission given to them. When I call upon the Lord in my morning quiet time, I ask Him for insight, energy, strength, and renewal of my mind and spirit. It is a deliberate choice I must make each day. My failure to do so results in senselessly sending myself into battle unarmed.

Lord, thank You for Your wisdom and divine providence. Without the Holy Spirit I am alone and so vulnerable. Help me make my prayer and Bible study time my number one priority daily. Amen.

FOLLOW THE LEADER

Read: Psalm 86

Teach me your way, O LORD,
and I will walk in your truth;
give me an undivided heart,
that I may fear your name.
I will praise you, O Lord my God,
with all my heart;
I will glorify your name forever.
PSALM 86:11–12

Happy childhood memories of playing "Follow the Leader" in our spacious backyard flood my mind. Hop on one foot. Now climb the little brick wall. Walk around the goldfish pond and run to the gate. Swing on the low branch of the mimosa tree. And so it went. We all knew the rules, but that is not to say we always followed them to the letter.

Life is full of rules, regulations, policies, and requirements. There are traffic laws and civil laws that help our society run in an orderly fashion. There are community rules governing building requirements that protect the interests of property owners. There are rules and policies that govern our workplaces. While the bureaucratic policies of the school board have at times seemed unnecessary to me, their intent is to provide order and enhance the quality of education.

God's rules are written for us in Exodus, chapter 20. Our Creator and heavenly Father did not set down the Ten Commandments to be oppressive or make life difficult. He provided them to remind the Israelites that He was the One ultimately in charge, and He wanted the best for His children.

David's prayer in Psalm 86 raises two important points regarding a good follower, especially of God. First, he asked God to teach him the way of truth. Like David, we need to be teachable. Just because we are teachers does not mean we have all of the answers! As we continue to learn new teaching methods and technological advances, we also must continue to learn the truths of God's Word. Learning is important, but application is critical for real understanding. It's like homework.

David also asked God to give him an "undivided heart." One of those great teacher phrases is "undivided attention." We want children to focus wholly on what we are saying. David recognized that many people and things competed for his attention and loyalty, but he knew to whom he should pledge 100 percent of his faith. Is there anything causing you to have a divided heart?

When we are teachable and totally devoted to God, then we are able to praise God with all of our hearts and bring glory and honor to Him.

Lord Jesus, help me to be teachable. Help me to focus on You and chart a steady course. Lord, I pray that my life will honor and glorify You. Amen.

BE STILL!

Read: Psalm 46

Be still, and know that I am God;
I will be exalted among the nations,
I will be exalted in the earth.
PSALM 46:10

When our son, Ben, was a toddler, he had a considerably large vocabulary and formed sentences very well. Of course, as a proud mother, I told all of my friends how well he talked. But when we would meet a friend in the mall or supermarket, Ben would clam up and not utter a word. Likewise, he could sit in front of a television without moving for an hour or more, but being still for a church service was out of the question!

In my relationship with God, I, too, can be less than compliant. My compulsion to overcommit myself causes me to end up exhausted, cranky, and dissatisfied. I allow myself to do so much "for God" that I forget to experience God.

But wait! Didn't God say "be still"? Why on earth would He want me to be still? Wouldn't He rather see me in action helping my neighbor, visiting the sick, or teaching a Bible class? Shouldn't I be planning for Vacation Bible School? What is wrong with being busy if I am doing good things?

God said to be still so that we can know Him. How did you get to know your best friend? You probably spent a lot of time just being together, talking and sharing from your heart. It took time to develop that personal relationship. When we meet and accept Jesus as our Savior, we can't just shake hands and say, "Nice to meet You, Jesus," and then go our way. God created you to fellowship with Him. He made you in His own image so He could communicate with you. Yes, we get to know God by talking with Him and spending time with Him.

We must also be still so we can *listen* to God. My mother was a patient woman, but she required our undivided attention when she spoke to us. "Look at me when I speak to you," she would demand of my brother and me. Similarly, God wants our undivided attention so He can speak to us. We must be purposefully still, listening for God's voice.

The Scripture also says to be still and worship God. The word *exalted* means to place above, to elevate to a place of honor. God will be exalted when we obey Him, when we serve His purposes and communicate with Him.

Being still, listening, communicating, and worshiping God will lead us to experiencing God. Worship God by being still and offering yourself totally to Him today.

Heavenly Father, I confess that my busyness may not be divinely ordered. Help me now to be still, totally focused on You and Your holiness. In the quiet of this moment, teach me Your will. Help me learn to worship You and know You more. Amen.

RETREATING AND RENEWING

Read: Matthew 14:22–23;
Romans 12:2

*Do not conform any longer
to the pattern of this world,
but be transformed by
the renewing of your mind.
Then you will be able to test
and approve what God's will is—
his good, pleasing and perfect will.*
ROMANS 12:2

As I sit here alone in the early morning on my brother-in-law's deck, I hear the birds singing and the squirrels chattering in a nearby thicket. The tranquility of the setting is refreshing, and I feel my inner well refilling. I need these quiet times to keep my life centered. I need these times for studying the Bible, reflecting on God's mercy, and contemplating what lies ahead. I can't go on without these spiritual mini-retreats.

Because Jesus was fully human, there were times when He grew weary and needed a quiet place of retreat. If the Lord recognized that need in His own life, surely we should also see it in ours. Your retreat may be in your favorite chair in the den before the rest of the family awakens. (I know this can be a challenge, especially when you have children to get dressed for day care or school.) Perhaps it's on the patio. Your quiet time and place may be in your classroom before everyone arrives. Where you meet God is your personal preference. The important point is to be sure to find a place to retreat and let yourself be renewed daily.

Without this ongoing renewal of our minds, Paul told the Romans that man could not know the will of God. This process keeps us centered in His will. We need to be refilled, renewed, and restored daily so we can be the men and women God calls us to be.

Dear Lord, I thank You for this time to sit and reflect on Your goodness and mercy. I need Your help to slow down and make time for daily devotions, Lord. I commit myself anew to You and ask You to renew my spirit and fill me with Your Holy Spirit. Amen.

NEED A CAVE?

Read: 1 Kings 19

When Elijah heard it,
he pulled his cloak over his face and
went out and stood at the mouth of the cave.
Then a voice said to him,
"What are you doing here, Elijah?"
The LORD said to him,
"Go back the way you came."
1 KINGS 19:13, 15

I have a new idea for turning a profit in my retirement years. I think I'll start a Rent-a-Cave business for people who need to get away from it all. No phones, no computers, no TV, just complete isolation. Clients' names would be held in strictest confidence to ensure their privacy.

Do you ever feel like the prophet Elijah and long for a cave? Do the burdens of being in the "Sandwich Generation" make you want to run away? Do financial pressures (mortgages, college tuition, unexpected car repairs, and so on) swamp you like a tidal wave? Does the pain and grief of losing someone leave you feeling desolate? Do the pressures of the classroom crash in on you? When I am faced with these circumstances, it is easy to lose my perspective and head for the hills (or caves) like Elijah. But when we look at what happened with Elijah, we can learn some valuable lessons to help us cope.

From a human standpoint, Elijah had every reason to run away. Far from a simple misdemeanor, he had just made the king and queen look foolish and had slaughtered all of their prophets. He was a wanted man! Yet, this once-bold fugitive who had confidently called upon God to consume the altar in fire was now fleeing like a coward. Why? In times of adversity, we have a tendency to forget God's promises. If we trust God in the good times, we should also trust Him when the going gets tough.

Second, God ministered to Elijah's needs

while he was in distress. Elijah ran into the desert and then lay down and prayed to die. Have you been so overwhelmed and emotionally spent that you did not think you could carry on? In Elijah's case, God sent angels to minister to Elijah with food and drink. Perhaps God has ministered to you through his earth angels (family and friends) who provided meals or sat at the hospital with your family member while you got some sleep. Maybe someone said just the right words to soothe you in a very dark and troubled time. Know that God will provide for your specific needs.

Third, God knew where Elijah was, but more importantly, he knew where Elijah needed to be. He didn't tell Elijah to stay in the cave, lick his wounds, and continue being fearful. God sent him back where he came from and gave him a new set of marching orders. Perhaps you, too, have discovered new ministry opportunities or a renewed sense of purpose following your visit to the cave.

My family has a motto: "Crises in three, way to be!" We rarely have one crisis occurring; they come like bananas in bunches. Yet, God continues to call me out of the cave and into His glorious light to find strength, hope, and a renewed sense of purpose. Trust God to lead you out of your cave, too.

Heavenly Father, Your love and providence never cease to amaze me. Thank You for ministering to me in times of distress and renewing my hope and strengthening me to carry on. Amen.

GOD'S CORRECTION FLUID

God has the power
   to cleanse and heal
   and make things right.
His grace covers my
   sins as correction fluid
   upon my life's theme.
His love covers my
   insecurities and
   inadequacies.
His strength hides
   my weaknesses
   and allows boldness
   with faith to shine through.

Yes, God's correction fluid
    can clean up my life, but
    His correction fluid is not
    white like snow.
It flows bloodred.
"Oh, precious is the flow
    That makes me white as snow
    No other fount I know
    Nothing but the blood of Jesus."*

*From "Nothing but the Blood"
by ROBERT LOWRY, *The Baptist Hymnal,* 1991,
Convention Press.

OH, SAY CAN YOU SEE?

Read: 2 Corinthians 4:1–4

*The god of this age has blinded
the minds of unbelievers,
so that they cannot see the light
of the gospel of the glory of Christ,
who is the image of God.*
2 CORINTHIANS 4:4

My first personal experience with sightless individuals was during my freshman year in college. Kathy and Mary lived in my dorm and were involved in some of the campus ministries. Both were astute young women who, despite their handicap, could stand their ground. After college, I met a visually handicapped couple through the church

I attended. Jim is completely blind, while Debbie has a small amount of vision in one eye. Like my college friends, they were intelligent, quick-witted, and blessed with a great sense of humor. But what I appreciated most about these individuals was their extraordinary vision.

While their visual acuity may have been destroyed, their spiritual vision was unhampered. They were neither blinded by the ways of this world nor persuaded by false teachings. Their spiritual vision was made possible by their commitment to Jesus Christ.

As you have read these devotionals, perhaps you have recognized that something is missing in your life. If you have not seen the glory of God in your life, I offer you this prescription for better vision:

1) Admit that you are a sinner.
   - Romans 3:23: "For all have sinned and fall short of the glory of God."
   - 1 John 1:9: "If we confess our sins, he is faithful and just and will forgive us our sins and purify us from all unrighteousness."

2) Believe that Jesus Christ, God's Son, died for you.
   - John 3:16: "For God so loved the world that he gave his one and only Son, that whoever believes in him shall not perish but have eternal life."

3) Confess that Jesus Christ is Lord.
   - Romans 10:9–10: That if you confess with your mouth, "Jesus is Lord," and believe in your heart that God raised him from the dead, you will be saved.
     For it is with your heart that you believe and are justified, and it is with your mouth that you confess and are saved.

If you can see your need to trust Jesus Christ, pray the following prayer now: "Lord Jesus, I invite You into my heart. I confess my sins and my need for Your saving grace. I believe that You died on the cross for me and rose again to give eternal life. Come into my heart and take control of my life now. Amen."

To keep your new vision clear, be sure to make prayer and Bible study a daily habit. Share your newfound faith with a Christian friend or pastor. Take time for fellowship with other Christians to help you learn and grow in the things of God.

MAY
GOD BLESS YOU
ALWAYS.

Inspirational Library

Beautiful purse/pocket-size editions of Christian classics bound in flexible leatherette. These books make thoughtful gifts for everyone on your list, including yourself!

When I'm on My Knees   The highly popular collection of devotional thoughts on prayer, especially for women.
Flexible Leatherette. $4.97

The Bible Promise Book   Over 1,000 promises from God's Word arranged by topic. What does God promise about matters like: Anger, Illness, Jealousy, Love, Money, Old Age, and Mercy? Find out in this book!
Flexible Leatherette. $3.97

Daily Wisdom for Women   A daily devotional for women seeking biblical wisdom to apply to their lives. Scripture taken from the New American Standard Version of the Bible.
Flexible Leatherette. $4.97

My Daily Prayer Journal   Each page is dated and features a Scripture verse and ample room for you to record your thoughts, prayers, and praises. One page for each day of the year.
Flexible Leatherette. $4.97

Available wherever books are sold.
Or order from:

Barbour Publishing, Inc.
P.O. Box 719
Uhrichsville, OH 44683
http://www.barbourbooks.com

If you order by mail, add $2.00 to your order for shipping.
Prices are subject to change without notice.